What people are

The Torch o~ ~..~..~~

As a devotee of Brighid and a flame tender for over thirty years, I was very happy to read this book. Erin Aurelia provides a beautiful, inspiring, and useful step-by-step guide to a devotional practice to the Goddess Brighid. She also offers an interesting new take on the Ogham fews which will be of interest even to those who have worked with Ogham before. Highly recommended.

Ellen Evert Hopman, author of *A Legacy of Druids - Conversations with Druid Leaders of Britain, the USA and Canada, Past and Present; A Druid's Herbal of Sacred Tree Medicine; the Druid trilogy of novels including Priestess of the Fire Temple - a Druid's Tale,* and other volumes

The Torch of Brighid is a fascinating and illuminating read. The path Erin Aurelia lays out, guided and inspired by the much-beloved goddess Brighid, offers wisdom, healing and spiritual transformation. Starting out on this journey has added new depth to my personal flametending practice and enriched my connection with Brighid. The guided meditations are beautifully written, and Aurelia's poetry simply shines.

Katrina Townsend, author of *The Anti-consumerist Druid*

The Torch of Brighid shines a new light on a path that many modern seekers of Brighid will feel drawn to pursue. In her book, Erin Aurelia presents an approach to Brighid that while modern in its form of expression, is inspired by authentic Irish traditions and lore surrounding the goddess and saint. This inspired practice merges various devotional forms, including – in a unique and innovative way – a weaving of the twenty

feda of tree ogham with the twenty days of the flame-tending cycle for Bighid. The Torch of Brighid is a beacon to a path that encourages both connecting to Irish traditions and a syncretic blending of them into a cohesive personal practice suited to seekers of Brighid from every culture around the world.
Daniela Simina, author of *Where Fairies Meet: Parallels between Irish and Romanian Fairy Traditions*

In The Torch of Brighid, Erin Aurelia – founder of the Daughters of Brighid Flametending Order – lays out a comprehensive devotional practice that synthesises several streams of traditional Irish wisdom to craft an innovative approach to flametending. Using the energies of the ogham alphabet as a guide to the vigil cycle of flametending, and integrating workings inspired by authentic Irish lore – including The Three Cauldrons of *The Cauldron of Poesy* and traditional prayers in honor of Brighid – this unique system shines with the illumination of Imbas, as is fitting for a spiritual practice intended to facilitate an ever-deepening relationship with Brighid, Irish Goddess of poetry, healing, and creativity. While this book is of particular benefit to the solitary practitioner who feels drawn to the work of tending Brighid's perpetual flame, the process outlined therein is complementary to other forms of flametending as well. Like a brilliant spark from Brighid's hammer, The Torch of Brighid forges a neoteric practice that both honors and is inspired by tradition.
Jhenah Telyndru (MA, Celtic Studies), author of *Rhiannon: Divine Queen of the Celtic Britons* and *Blodeuwedd: Welsh Goddess of Seasonal Sovereignty*

The Torch of Brighid

Flametending for Transformation

The Torch of Brighid

Flametending for Transformation

Erin Aurelia

**MOON
BOOKS**

Winchester, UK
Washington, USA

JOHN HUNT PUBLISHING

First published by Moon Books, 2023
Moon Books is an imprint of John Hunt Publishing Ltd., No. 3 East Street, Alresford
Hampshire SO24 9EE, UK
office@jhpbooks.net
www.johnhuntpublishing.com
www.moon-books.net

For distributor details and how to order please visit the 'Ordering' section on our website.

ISBN: 978 1 78904 281 8
978 1 78904 916 9 (ebook)
Library of Congress Control Number: 2022938653

A CIP catalogue record for this book is available from the British Library.

Design: Matthew Greenfield

UK: Printed and bound by CPI Group (UK) Ltd, Croydon, CR0 4YY
Printed in North America by CPI GPS partners

We operate a distinctive and ethical publishing philosophy in
all areas of our business, from our global network of authors to
production and worldwide distribution.

Contents

To the past, present, and future Flametenders

Acknowledgements

Many thanks to everyone who supported and encouraged me on this writing adventure as I spent a year writing this book with one foot in this world and one in the Otherworld.

Thanks to all my Patreon supporters and beta readers for their invaluable support and feedback, especially to patrons and friends Josephine and Christopher Pizzarello for their generous patronage and belief in me, and to beta readers and friends Cara Silla and Jennifer Hughes for their thorough feedback and emotional support. Y'all are the best; much love to each of you!

Thanks to Moon Books editor Trevor Greenfield for his interest in my project and assistance in bringing it to the publisher. I am honored to be part of the Moon Books family of authors.

Thanks to all my flametending sisters in both the Nigheanan Brìghde (NB) and Daughters of the Flame (DoF) flametending orders. I am grateful for all the love and support I received from my sisters in NB during the eight years that I created and led the order, sharing these practices as they came to me at that time. And I am also grateful to the sisterhood of the DoF for providing a safe landing space when my life upended, when I could only tend Brighid's flame in solitude and silence to rest and heal. As I healed, the fullness of this practice came to me.

Regarding the poems I share herein, I'd like to extend special thanks to my local community of open-mic poets and musicians who have supported and encouraged me since I found them a few years ago. You all gave me a place to find the power in my voice and I wouldn't be who I am today without any of you. Thank you all for always listening to and hearing me. Performing with and for you all is one of my greatest joys!

Finally, I offer deep gratitude to Brighid herself, Goddess of the Three-Fold Fire of Poetry, Healing, and Smithcraft, for her constant presence and guidance over the past twenty years.

Thank you for your steady light illuminating what I needed to see, warming me in the dark, walking me to wholeness, and filling my head with your fire of inspiration. May your light reach all who are searching for what you can provide. *Gabhaim molta Brighide*.

Preface

To properly orient you, dear reader, to the nature of this book, I must clarify what this book is not doing, and what it intends to do. For those of you new to pagan traditions, this will give you an idea of what various pagan books can do, and set this one within that scope of possibilities. For those of you who are longtime practitioners of pagan traditions, you will understand my aims in making this statement and why I am doing so.

This book is not

- reconstructing a past pagan practice, as there is no known pre-Christian flametending practice to Brighid which *can* be reconstructed
- speculating that the unorthodox mystic connections made herein are supported by the lore, or should be
- claiming any historicity for the practice it outlines
- suggesting that the practice outlined herein is any singular or proper way to flametend above any other
- stating that the ogham was or is in any way mythically connected to Brighid, or should be

This book is

- presenting an inspired practice, like spiritual poetry
- making imaginative mythic connections based on thematic resonance to be used as meaningful tools for spiritual development
- suggesting that combining the twenty nights of flametending with a journey through the twenty feda of the ogham can provide a unique and creative process for engaging with the devotional practice of flametending

for Brighid in order to foster spiritual development with Brighid as a guide
- a product of imbas, or inspiration, inspired by Brighid, goddess of imbas herself
- hopefully an inspiration to you too, dear reader, as, like Brighid's perpetual Fire, imbas is a flame that grows when shared
- an offering from my spirit to yours

Thank you for choosing to read my book. I hope this practice nourishes your soul as it has mine while I developed it, and as it does when I practice it.

Brighid Bless,

Erin Aurelia

What She Speaks When I Tend Her Flame
by Erin Aurelia

I transform, she says:

the raw meat into food
the raw thoughts into poetry
the raw materials into arts and crafts
the raw ore into weapons and tools
the raw plants into healing draughts

in your heart, distress to peace

in your mind, worry to reassurance

in your body, death into life, then life into growth

in your life, suffering into power

I transform, by the grace of the flame

She said, you too can embody transformation:
from chaos to order
from complacency to vigilance
from disease to healing
from loneliness to togetherness
from otherworlds to thisworld
from outside to in
from self to others
like a gift

gifting is gracing

gift yourself, gift another, and then another
receive in grace, give in grace,
become grace

and then, we
become the Flame,
her flame in this world

so shine on:
for her, for you, for all

Discovering the Transformational Flametending Journey

I first met Brighid during a Reiki attunement, a ritual process of becoming attuned to perform a form of hands-on energy healing. In the blast of hot, healing energy that coursed through my body as my chakras were opened to receive it, what I saw and felt was Brighid's bright flame, and its heat charged me like electricity. In that moment, I learned that her fire transforms those who become filled with it. Shortly after that, I became a flametender for Brighid and have been tending her Eternal Flame for twenty years.

These twenty years have seen several iterations of my life and practice come and go, but Brighid has remained constant through them all. Her burning torch lit and guided my way, and where she led, I followed. I followed her from being one who burned myself out for others to one who learned to tend her flame from within. I followed her in my spiritual practices from celebration to devotion to contemplation to transformation. I followed her to the traditions of my ancestors and to their Well of Memory, where they sang their songs to me in new arrangements and asked me to sing them to the world for them. The practice I am sharing in these pages is one such song.

I always looked forward to and enjoyed my flametending vigils. They were times for communion with Brighid, for sitting in and being held by her energy. She both soothed and vitalized me. After many years of tending her flame, I longed for some more frequent regular practice for communing with her, not only every twenty days, as run the flametending vigils. I also craved more regular fellowship with Brighid devotees than I was experiencing in the order I was tending with at the time.

I began meditating with her on weekends and inviting others to join from a distance, after which we could share experiences together online. Despite great interest, few participated. As I deepened into both my flametending practice and learning more about Gaelic tradition, I decided to create a flametending order that would include all the elements I was searching for: vital community, daily interaction, and creation of meditations and rituals. I founded the Nigheanan Brìghde Flametending Order, or the Daughters of Brighid Flametending Order, which I tended for eight years.

During those years, Brighid inspired me to develop guided meditations to use during flametending vigils, seasonal feasts, and lunar phases. Then she showed me a synchronicity that became the template for a whole new way to practice flametending: the way that the twenty days of the flametending cycle match with the twenty letters of the traditional Irish tree ogham alphabet, in which each alphabet letter is denoted by a tree and infused with esoteric meaning. Enthralled and excited, I began communing with Brighid daily, guided by the energies of the daily tree that correlated with the current day of the flametending cycle. I wrote prayers to Brighid and recited them to her daily, asking for her support in finding the wisdom each tree had to offer for each day.

After some time in this iteration of my practice, I began to view the ogham, commonly used today as a form of divination, as not only a collection of trees and their esoterica, but like the major arcana of the tarot, a depiction of a spiritual journey of transformation. I saw this journey of transformation as akin to the journey of the life cycle of a tree seed through the seasons, with a growth, a flowering, a fruiting, and finally a seeding to begin the cycle anew. I observed that the trees that opened each of the four classes of the trees of the ogham correlated with trees that aligned with the four seasons. I understood that these seasons reflected the maturation of the spirit through the journey of transformation and the gleaning of wisdom which then informed the journey of the next cycle, so that transformation built on itself in never-ending spirals of inner alchemy. And through what I have seen, I have developed a daily practice for spiritual transformation that is guided by Brighid each step of the way, as she has guided me in its creation.

Through practicing each iteration of this path as I developed it, I came to learn that growth is not only made through obtaining wisdom, but by implementing it. And Brighid showed me that I can effectively implement it by embodying her own skills as Shaper, Healer, Seer, and Transformer. Through embodying her skills, I became empowered and took a hand in steering my own inner growth. This power grew within me and was fueled by Brighid's own Eternal Fire. I came to understand that flametending is not only a practice kept with candles for her at our shrines, but also kept with the inner work of keeping alight the bright light our souls, which can be supported by Brighid's own light. And as my soul was supported by Brighid's fire, I was transformed, as is everything that is touched by fire. I transformed from one who was shaped by outside forces to a Shaper, from one who was sapped of energy to a Healer, and from one who was confused to a Seer who saw and understood the signs of wisdom and how to use them to tend my own soul flame, to understanding that this is the inner essence of temporal flametending.

Please note that while this book draws on several elements of Irish tradition, the practice outlined herein is not traditional in itself, but inspired. I hope it will, in turn, inspire you to follow the light of Brighid's torch in search of your inner transformation. I suggest reading the book through before beginning its practice, and following its practice as written for a while before altering it to suit your personal taste. These exercises and meditations are powerful and will continue working within you even after you have ended your vigil for the day. When the practice has become familiar, then Brighid may begin guiding you in new directions most relevant to your own spiritual development at that time.

As flametenders, we not only tend her flame but are guided by it, and she always guides us to just what we most need. Transformation never ends and its winding path can take many forms. There is no destination, just the winding path with the steady company of Brighid and the guiding torch of her Eternal Fire. Enjoy the journey.

The Three-Fold Fire of Brighid

Fire in the forge that shapes and tempers
Fire in the cauldron that nourishes and heals
Fire in the head that incites and inspires

-attributed to the Ord Brighideach flametending order

Chapter 1

The History of Tending Brighid's Perpetual Fire

Flametending is the sacred service of tending Brighid's Perpetual Fire. No one is certain when the practice began, but the place where it began was an abbey, later a cathedral, called *Cill Dara*, or Church of the Oak. It was founded by a young Christian woman named Brigit in Ireland's Kingdom of Leinster in the year 480 BCE. The practice of flametending there is documented in the twelfth century by Gerald of Wales in his tome, *The History and Topography of Ireland*, which he wrote when he toured Ireland shortly after its conquest by the Normans some six centuries after Brigit's time. He writes:

> *AT Kildare, in Leinster, celebrated for the glorious Brigit, many miracles have been wrought worthy of memory. Among these, the first that occurs is the fire of St. Brigit, which is reported never to go out. Not that it cannot be extinguished, but the nuns and holy women tend and feed it, adding fuel, with such watchful and diligent care, that from the time of the Virgin, it has continued burning through a long course of years; and although such heaps of wood have been consumed during this long period, there has been no accumulation of ashes.*
>
> *As in the time of St. Brigit twenty nuns were here engaged in the Lord's warfare, she herself being the twentieth, after her glorious departure, nineteen have always formed the society, the number having never been increased. Each of them has the care of the fire for a single night in turn, and, on the evening before the twentieth night, the last nun, having heaped wood upon the fire, says, 'Brigit, take charge of your own fire; for this night belongs to you.' She then leaves the fire, and. in the morning it is found that the fire has not*

5

gone out, and that the usual quantity of fuel has been used. THIS fire is surrounded by a hedge, made of stakes and brushwood, and forming a circle, within which no male can enter; and if anyone should presume to enter, which has been sometimes attempted by rash men, he will not escape the divine vengeance. Moreover, it is only lawful for women to blow the fire, fanning it or using bellows only, and not with their breath.

No other documented accounts of the tradition exist. History, alas, did not permit Brighid's Perpetual Flame to live up to its perpetual status. In 1220 CE, about a century after Gerald of Wales's visit, the Archbishop of Dublin declared the practice pagan and, to suppress superstition, officially had the flame extinguished. Later after his death, the nuns rekindled it. Roughly four centuries later though, during the Reformation, King Henry VIII sought to eradicate popery and ordered all the monasteries throughout England and Ireland closed, and so the flame was again extinguished in the early 1500s, where it remained dark for roughly another four hundred years.

Then, in 1993, Brighid's Perpetual Flame auspiciously re-entered the world in two different locations on Brighid's feast day, February 1st, by parties unaware of their cosmic synchronicity. In Kildare's Market Square, Mary Teresa Cullen and the Catholic Brigidine Sisters rekindled Brighid's Flame during an international conference being held there titled, Brigid: Prophetess, Earthwoman, Peacemaker. Meanwhile, across an ocean and a continent to the west, in Vancouver, British Columbia, Canada, Mael Brigde and a small group of neopagan women gathered to rekindle Brighid's Flame and officially form a modern flametending order in the tradition recorded by Gerald of Wales to re-establish the custom of flametending for Brighid. They called their order the Daughters of the Flame.

In the following years, a member of the Daughters of the Flame formed another neopagan flametending order, Ord Brighideach, or The Order of Brighid, to welcome flametenders of all genders from around the globe, and Brighid's Perpetual Flame blazed even brighter in the world.

In 2014, Clann Bhríde, or the Children of Brighid, was founded by a small group of people who joined forces to create a structured religious practice devoted to the Celtic goddess Brighid and Her Mysteries, to which they added a virtual flametending order for all genders in 2015. While Brighid's Perpetual Flame is housed and tended today in Solas Bhríde, the home of the Brigidine Sisters, the North American-founded orders gather online in virtual groups in which members tend Brighid's flame during their assigned night and day in their homes on altars and shrines dedicated to the goddess and saint.

Today, the Brigidine Sisters tend the Perpetual Flame in the town of Kildare at their Solas Bhríde center. On their website, they tell us that:

A sacred fire burned in Kildare reaching back into pre-Christian times. Scholars suggest that priestesses used to gather on the hill of Kildare to tend their ritual fires while invoking a goddess named Brigid to protect their herds and to provide a fruitful harvest.
When St. Brigid built her monastery and church in Kildare, she continued the custom of keeping the fire alight. For her and her nuns the fire represented the new light of Christianity, which reached our shores early in the fifth century.

Any texts which might have recorded the pre-Christian flametending tradition at Kildare have failed to survive, but nevertheless, conjecture of a pre-Christian practice persists, alongside the suggestion that the abbey and cathedral of Kildare were constructed atop a pre-existing pagan temple dedicated to the pre-Christian Irish goddess, Brighid. In the thirteenth century, a cathedral was built where the abbey was founded which remains today, and the foundation of its original fire temple, said to be used by Brighid and her nuns for flametending, was restored in 1988 and adorned with a plaque reading, *St. Brigid's Fire Temple.*

Brighid's Perpetual Fire has proved irrepressible and indeed promises to only grow brighter over the coming decades. People the world over are drawn to this practice of honoring Brighid, whether goddess or saint, to seek solace, healing, inspiration, and guidance from this numinous power, and to keep Brighid's energy alive in our world through physically lighting and contemplatively tending her flame.

Connecting with and flametending for Brighid every twenty nights is a beautiful devotional practice. I've also found, through Brighid's guidance, that deep spiritual transformation can transpire through tending Brighid's flame during all twenty nights of the traditional flametending cycle, thereby creating a nourishing daily meditation practice.

When combined with ogham work, an illuminated path appears, lit by Brighid's guiding torch, which one has only to follow to discover another mystery of flametending: tending the flame within. This inner flame is also lit by Brighid and resonates with the same creative power of the Universe which at once shapes, balances, and enlightens, then dissolves to return to Source to be used to shape anew. If you revere Brighid, you can construct her Church of the Oak within yourself to house and tend your perpetual spiritual light so it may inspire and strengthen you, and then through you, further illuminate the world with the gifts of Brighid's Perpetual Fire.

Chapter 2

The Inner Alchemy of the Flametending Journey

Why We Journey: Spiritual Transformation

This book is for devotees of Brighid and those curious about Brighid and the flametending tradition who seek a deep practice of spiritual exploration and growth guided by Brighid's light and wisdom. The depths can be dark, but her torch ever shines to illuminate a way for us toward our own illumination, healing, and growth. The practice in these pages is an invitation to follow this lit path through the forest of ogham trees in search of your true self, your unbreakable and remarkable soul hiding behind and beneath your fears. Just as the smiths, healers, and poets who revered Brighid were once considered magicians, through following this practice, you will learn to embody these spiritual skills of Brighid and practice alchemy on your own spirit as you turn the lead of fear and illusion into the gold of power and wisdom.

As it is the nature of all life to grow and change, so too is it the nature of our souls. They grow and change through lived experiences. When we learn, or become enlightened in some matter, we grow, and growth is a change, which is transformation. This can readily happen to us while minding our daily business and getting on with living our mundane lives, so why take on spiritual transformation as a conscious pursuit? Because spiritual growth accelerates when we do so, which develops our inner power and strength. With greater power and strength, we attain greater vision and become stronger vessels for receiving and containing wisdom that in turn help us to make more mindful choices, which brings spiritual abundance to ourselves and subsequently to our world. When we transform, our world transforms, and when we receive abundance, we then have riches to share with the world. Spiritual growth is a positive feedback loop that brings more and more abundance, spiraling out from our inner spiritual sanctuaries into everything around us, and this received abundance of inspiration, vision, healing, and wisdom will shine from you like a torch for others, warming and guiding their souls as yours is warmed and guided by Brighid. When we consciously step into spiritual transformation, we become Brighid's torch for those around us, and in this way, keep her fire alight in the world. This is the soul of flametending.

Our Guide: Brighid of Wisdom

Brighid is beloved and renown in Ireland as both a Pagan goddess and a Catholic saint. As the sacred fire that shapes, heals and inspires, she is essentially the force that transforms: the raw ore into tools and weapons, raw meat into food, raw plants into medicine, and raw ideas into visionary works of art rich with meaning. As the goddess and saint is associated in Ireland and Scotland with the arrival of the season of spring, hers is also the transforming fire radiating both up from the depths of the earth and down from the shining sun that renews the power of the land and its growth. Reflecting this understanding inward, she also speaks to the inner alchemy of spiritual transformation that brings her light of illumination to our darkest places where the lower energies trapped there can be transformed into meaningful insight and cosmic vision. She is at once the carrier and the embodiment of the perpetual flame that guides, inspires, and enlightens so many.

Examining mythic and historic information about Brighid reveals commonalities between this goddess and saint of the same name. Continental Celticist Henri d'Arbois de Jubainville claims in his 1884 work, *Le Cycle Mythologique Irlandais et la Mythologie Celtique*, that,

...Brigit, goddess of the pagan Irish, was supplanted in the Christian era by Saint Brigit, and the Irish of the Middle Ages transferred in some way to this national saint the cult that their pagan ancestors had addressed to the goddess Brigit.

While no Irish accounts exist articulating that the people of Ireland deliberately transformed their Pagan goddess into a Catholic saint, de Jubainville's passage has inspired the sentiment among many in contemporary Ireland and abroad. Both the goddess and the saint are also known in Scotland, Wales, the Isle of Man, and England. Brighid's name in modern Irish is spelled *Bríd*, and depending on dialect, pronounced BREED or BREEDJ.

In James MacKillop's 1998 *Dictionary of Celtic Mythology*, his entry, "Brigit," begins,

Pre-Christian Irish goddess of fire, smithing, fertility, cattle, crops, and poetry.

She was the goddess of those primal elements which had supported Ireland's Iron-Age Celtic society, where fire was the cultural crux. With fire, mined ore could be fashioned into tools, which allowed the early farmers to break up the land and plant crops. Harvested grains could then feed both the people and their cattle over the winter, allowing them to build settlements. Fire baked their grains into bread. And once settled, with food secured, the communal and hearth fires were sanctuaries around which the people gathered, where culture could flourish, and mythic tales were shared to remind the people who they were and what their role was in the cosmos where they dwelled with the many other beings of the living world. And the fires of the smithy also forged weapons with which warriors could defend the people and their settlements.

Sometime during the ninth century, an entry was made in *Cormac's Glossary*, a large collection of rare Irish words and historical and mythological names, under "Brigit," reading:

Brigit i.e., a poetess, daughter of the Dagda. This is Brigit the female sage, or woman of wisdom, i.e., Brigit the goddess whom poets adored, because very great and very famous was her protecting care. It is therefore they call her goddess of poets by this name. Whose sisters were Brigit the female physician [woman of leechcraft,] Brigit the female smith [woman of smithwork]; from whose names with all Irishmen a goddess was called Brigit.

Here, we see that, even more than a goddess serving as the central axis of society, Brighid was known as a sage, a goddess of wisdom, whose power was also evident by her protection of the poets who worshiped her, the poets being the keepers of societal wisdom who reminded the people who they were. Her father, the Dagda, was the father of the tribe of the gods, the Tuatha dé Danann, and keeper of the Cauldron of Plenty which never emptied, and from whom no one ever went away hungry. He is revered today by many contemporary Pagans as the Irish god of druidism, or traditional Irish occult wisdom. So Brighid inherited these elements of fertility and wisdom from her father. She is also noted as having two sisters, where we find Brighid the Smith and Brighid the Physician, or Healer, providing the source for our present-day understanding of her as a triple-goddess of the aforementioned three domains. Interestingly, the name Brigit is also given as another word for goddess, suggesting that, more than a name, Brighid may be a title. The root of her name, *brig*, means, "exalted," denoting Brighid as, "The Exalted One."

The Iron-Age Celts of Ireland celebrated four primary feast days which denoted their four seasons. The feast day celebrated in early February was called Imbolc to acknowledge the arrival of spring, fertility's reawakening with the lengthening of the days and the first appearance of new vegetation. Livestock was bred in early November to be prepared to give birth at this time so the mothers could feed on the new growth to produce milk for their young. MacKillop notes in his entry titled, "Imbolc" that,

> From earliest times Imbolc was associated with Brigit, the fire-goddess, and after Christianization with St. Brigid of Kildare, eventually becoming known as St. Brigid's Day.

St. Brigid's Day is still celebrated today in Ireland and abroad on the first of February, as is the festival of Imbolc, to honor both the goddess and the saint, and the resurrection of spring from the darkness and death of winter.

Brigid, later St. Brigid, was likely born in Ireland's County Louth in the middle of the fifth century. Little is known about Brigid the woman, but fantastical tales and miracles of her life are recorded in a Latin biography titled, *Vita Brigitae*, or *The Life of Brigid*, compiled around the year 650CE by a cleric named Cogitosus. The story of her parentage and birth is striking – her father was said to be a druid, and her mother his maid who gave birth to her at sunrise on the threshold of his home, neither inside nor out, upon which a blaze of fiery light shone from the babe's head up to the heavens. Her first diet was equally notable, as she would only take the milk of white, red-eared cow, whose coloring indicates she was of otherworldly origin. Tales tell of her being a generous and feisty girl, giving away her father's belongings and food to strangers in need, and later, when he tried to marry her off, she instead poked out one of her eyes with a stick to mar her beauty so she'd no longer be desirable. Afterward, she restored her own sight and chose to dedicate her life to God. She was said to have once converted a man on his deathbed by telling him the story of Christ and weaving a cross out of rushes from the floor as she did so, which later became commemorated on her feast day with the custom of weaving these Brigid's Crosses to hang up in the home for the holiday.

They are traditionally hung over doorways to protect families and placed in byres to protect livestock, as the saint is associated with the lambs popularly born on her day.

A popular tale tells that Brigid desired to form a Christian church and community, so went to the King of Leinster to request land upon which to build a monastery. When he refused, she told him, "Give me just as much land as my cloak will cover." Laughing, he readily agreed, whereupon Brighid instructed four of her accompanying friends to each take hold of and pull on the four corners of her cloak. As they did so, to the amazement of the King and his company, the cloak magically grew until it covered an expanse of fields, as well as the nearby lake and wood, and there, beside an oak tree, she built her abbey.

Interestingly, the word *druid* stems from the word *dara*, meaning "oak," after which Brighid named her abbey, which further connects Ireland's Pagan past with its Christian present, and the Pagan goddess Brighid with the Catholic saint.

The Path: The Tree Ogham

Another known Irish artifact numbering to twenty, like the nights of the flametending cycle, is the *ogham* (pronounced, OH-um). Ogham is a primitive Irish script containing twenty letters (and a later addition of five more letters) in which each is connected to several associations based on items beginning with the sound of the letter. There are several collections of these, grouped into and named for various subjects, such as color ogham or bird ogham, for example. These names and collections were used as mnemonic devices to help learners remember the letters. The most popular collection is called the tree ogham, in which each letter is named for a tree and carries various cultural and spiritual meanings.

The tree ogham begins with the letter called *Beith*, associated with the birch tree. As the first letter, Beith carries spiritual meanings of birth and initiation, providing apt guidance for stepping into a spiritual journey. The last letter of the tree alphabet is *Idad*, known by the yew tree. Idad connotes endings not only by way of ending the ogham alphabet, but by also being a tree heavily associated with death, as it was commonly planted in graveyards. Death infers transformation, a change from one form to another. Our spirituality is a key component of our energetic makeup and just as energy is neither created nor destroyed but merely changes form, so does our spirit transform when one stage of its expression is transcended, and moves into another, higher level. Birth, death, and rebirth create a cycle of flowing energy that transmutes one level of understanding into another.

The ogham script dates from at least the fifth century CE. Its collection of twenty letters is referred to as the *feda*, or the woods, referring to trees and shrubs associated with its letters. The tree letters are arranged in four groups called *aicmí*, or classes. There is also a fifth class called the *forfeda*, created later after the original set of twenty, which was intended to introduce new sounds to the Irish language that were not native to it. They are also each associated with a tree or shrub.

This form of writing was not heavily employed, and was primarily chiseled into standing stones, bone, or amber to either mark boundaries, make ceremonial inscriptions, or, occasionally, create a magical amulet. The letters were carved up along a straight vertical edge or on a created line, from bottom to top.

According to *The Book of Ogams*, a seventh century primer for Irish poets describing the ogham, the letters were also used by the learned or druidic class to pass silent messages between them by a sort of sign language in which the letters would be formed with the fingers against the straight edge of either the shin bone, nose, or the side of the hand. They also used the ogham in some noted divination methods, such as to determine if a fetus in utero was male or female. This book is found within a lengthier handbook called *The Scholar's Primer*, which is again contained within the larger manuscript called *The Book of Ballymote*. In *The*

Scholar's Primer, an origin tale of the ogham is told in which the alphabet was created by Ogma, the Irish god of eloquence and poetry, when he wanted to leave a roadside message for the god Lugh to warn him that his wife was in danger. Brighid, Ogma, and Lugh are all members of the *Tuatha dé Danann*, or People of the Goddess Dana, the old gods of Ireland said to be masters of all the arts and sciences.

Brighid being a goddess of poetry then segues well with a system of writing mythically created by a fellow deity of poetry containing spiritual as well as utilitarian functions that was used by the druidic class, who were the poets and philosophers of the ancient Irish tribes. Today the ogham is primarily used by neodruids and neopagans for divination, and sometimes for ceremonial or secret writing. In this flametending practice, the ogham becomes the roadmap of the transformational journey, traveled one tree at a time during each of the twenty flametending vigils, into the forest the deep self, guided by Brighid's bright torch of wisdom.

This journey can be metaphorically understood by viewing the entire process of growth and transformation from Beith to Idad and perceiving its four classes as stages of that process. These stages can be visualized as the four seasons and their effect on a fruiting deciduous tree, which can then be allegorically correlated with four distinct stages of spiritual development.

The first class can correlate with spring and spiritual formation, the shaping of a spiritual focus. The second class can correlate with summer and fruiting, and with spiritual examination, seeking balance in the consciously formed spirit. The third class can correlate with autumn and ripening, and with spiritual illumination, harvesting wisdom from the spirit's balance. And the fourth class correlate with winter and spiritual transformation, in which the wisdom gleaned is distilled to its essence and retained within to inform future experiences, the same way the life energy of a tree is distilled in its seeds so they can generate new trees. The practice of flametending for transformation leads the flametender through each of these stages over the course of twenty nights to effect the inner alchemy of revelation.

The Mythic Template: The Oak of Mugna, Irish Tree of Knowledge

Along with the oak tree St. Brigit's abbey, Cill Dara (later anglicized as Kildare), was founded beside and named after, another nearby and notable oak tree in Irish lore is the legendary Oak of Mugna. It's one of the five mythic guardian trees of Ireland, one planted in each of Ireland's five provinces. These sacred trees are noted in the tale called The Settling of the Manor of Tara, found in the medieval Irish manuscript, *The Yellow Book of Lecan*. In this tale, a mysterious giant appeared at the royal palace of Tara during an important gathering who explained to Ireland's high king how Ireland came to be divided into those provinces. This giant arrived bearing a branch that contained acorns, hazelnuts, and apples that he said was descended from the Tree of Knowledge of the Garden of Eden.

After he shared his story with the high king and the poets, he gave the branch to an old wise man and told him to plant five of its seeds around the island of Ireland. These trees became the mythic guardian trees of Ireland's provinces, which symbolized their vitality and prosperity, and under which tribal chieftains were coronated to legitimate their rule. The Oak of Mugna is the tree that grew in the eastern province of Leinster, where County Kildare is located. It was the only one of the five guardian trees that also fruited threefold in acorns, hazelnuts, and apples as the original branch did. They are all associated with wisdom in Celtic traditions, which is what conscious transformation yields. Because Brighid is a goddess of wisdom, there is a thematic resonance between her and this mythic tree, and through this resonance, we can engage with the Oak of Mugna as a facilitator of spiritual transformation within this Brighidine flametending practice.

These two legendary oak trees associated in different ways

with Brighid both denote a connection with spiritual wisdom. In a practice of spiritual development, Cill Dara, the Church or Sanctuary of the Oak, named for the tree growing where Brighid built her abbey, was built can metaphorically represent inner growth, thereby suggesting an inner sanctuary. And as the abbey of Cill Dara tended a sacred flame, so too can the inner sanctuary within each of us tend a spiritual reflection of this physical sacred flame, which are in turn both iterations of the greater fire at the center of the earth that is its creative and transformative life force. Further, the earth's inner flame is also a microcosm of the macrocosmic creative energy of the sun and the entire cosmos. As each flame is connected by resonance, the practice of flametending connects us with the power of them all.

Not only do these flames connect with each other across space and connect our inner world with our daily lives, a mythic reflection and relationship can be drawn between these flames and the greater container of the living universe, which in the Irish tradition comprises both the seen physical world and the unseen Otherworld. Irish tradition holds that what presents itself to us in our physical world first manifests itself in the mythic Otherworld. Therefore, the physical fire burning had its first in the mythic realm, which is considered the origin of primal energy, and what supports it in our world. In this way, the Otherworld can be considered the primal cosmic source of Brighid's Perpetual Fire, and so tending it connects us with the Otherworld too, along with its spiritual gifts.

The mythic Oak of Mugna can be engaged with as the otherworldly energy that fuels the physical oak tree growing at Cill Dara, or as the tree behind the tree, an Irish saying referring to each physical form's unseen imprint of spiritual energy surrounding it.

While this transformational flametending journey follows the path of the ogham, its transformational process follows the life cycle of the Oak of Mugna as it progresses through the four seasons. The path and the process work in tandem. As the story of the Oak of Mugna develops on the mythic plane, through focused meditational work correlating with each developmental stage, your soul subsequently develops on the spiritual plane. The life cycle of the mythic tree's sprouted seed from sapling, to flowering tree, to fruiting tree, to fallen fruit sowing seeds to begin the cycle again creates the mythic template for this transformational flametending process. In this way, your spiritual work connects your inner development with both cosmic and mythic cycles of life, death, and rebirth, and the wisdom these cycles impart.

The spiritual development of our inner soul sanctuary is also fed by the mythic development of the Oak of Mugna and the energy generated during this practice's spiritual work, which results in spiritual expansion along with transformation.

The Power Centers: The Cauldron of Poesy

As Brighid was known primarily as a goddess of poetry, and the spiritual meaning of the ogham letters is spoken in the symbolic language of poetry, the Irish manuscript speaking to the art of poetry and poetic inspiration reasonably bears on this flametending work. This manuscript is known as The Cauldron of Poesy and speaks to energy centers within the body similar in concept to what other traditions refer to as chakras. The guidance found herein prepares the body, mind, and spirit for the deep spiritual healing work of the flametending journey.

The manuscript discusses poetic inspiration as arising and flowing through the poet through three internal, esoteric energy centers, conceived of as cauldrons, located within, and formed by, the three cavities of the skeletal structure: the pelvic region, the thoracic region, and the cranial region. Like inner bowls, they contain, or potentially contain *imbas*, the spiritual fire of inspiration. In order to receive and hold this energy, these inner cauldrons must be sitting right side up, but they are not all said to do so in a person upon birth. Spiritual work must turn them all the right way. Once they are righted, inspiration as illumination and articulation develop within the poet and the insight is spoken as poetry. Flametenders can similarly utilize this energy of imbas for spiritual learning and growth, as, like the poet's, the transformational flametender's journey is one of illumination.

Each inner cauldron has a name pertaining to its particular operation and function within this overall system. The first, in the pelvic region, is called the Cauldron of Warming. In the Irish manuscript, it is said to be always upright within a person, as it is the seat of the primal physical energy that powers the body and stimulates the basic learning of our youth. The second cauldron, in the thoracic center within our ribcage, is called the Cauldron of Motion. This one is said to be originally sitting on its side, or tipped on its lip when we are born, so must be turned upright to be activated. This turning, or motion, is accomplished through strong emotions of sorrow and joy; interesting, as it sits at the heart center. Once it is turned upright, the third cauldron in the cranial cavity of the skull can be accessed, called the Cauldron of Knowledge, where illumination is attained. This cauldron is said to be face-down in all persons at birth, so is the one most challenging to successfully overturn.

Because strong emotions are the key force which overturn the central, and in the manuscript, most prominent cauldron, the Cauldron of Motion (or Vocation, referencing the vocation of the poet), deep emotional processing and healing are required, so is foundational to spiritual growth. Though some spiritual traditions regard emotions as undesirable or distracting, the Irish tradition resolutely embraces them as intrinsic to the human experience, as well as powerful gateways to spiritual illumination. This acceptance extends even to those emotions commonly regarded as negative, including anger, grief, and jealousy, as well as love, sexual ecstasy, and divine grace, as all are capable of guiding, teaching, and developing us into whole persons. Activating these inner cauldrons both opens us up to the spiritual work of the flametending journey, and once turned, catalyzes and contains the powers of inspiration and illumination as we progress along the journey.

The flametender in this practice can further conceptualize these cauldrons as sources of Brighid's power to guide their way. The Cauldron of Warming can be engaged with as Brighid the Smith's forge, stoking the fire of our physical energy. The Cauldron of Motion can be engaged with as Brighid the Healer's cauldron of tonic herbal infusions on the hearth fire, supporting our deep emotional work. And the Cauldron of Knowledge can be conceived of as Brighid the Poet's Well of Wisdom from which the fire of imbas arises and transforms spiritual energy into illumination.

Chapter 3

Preparation for the Flametending Journey

Now it's time for you to prepare your space and yourself for your transformational flametending journey. Because transformational work is done and occurs within, this preparation work creates both a shrine and special candle for Brighid in the physical world for your flametending and an inner fire temple in the spiritual plane for this deep communion, to mirror your space in the physical world. You will also visit Brighid's Well of Wisdom to discover how your transformational flametending journey will begin, then learn an energy practice for opening your power centers to receive and attune with the energy of Brighid and fortify you as you commune with her.

Undertake these steps as you are able to make time for them. Though they may each only take an hour of your time at most, make sure you won't be rushed through them by other pressing engagements weighing on you. These steps may be completed in a day or a week, however you have time for them. Take them in order and give each your full attention.

Through performing the following ritual, exercise, and meditations, your physical life will become aligned with your inner spiritual world, and their resonance will create one cohesive world whose outer and inner dimensions will harmoniously vibrate and operate as one to support you in your transformational flametending practice.

First you will create a physical shrine and flametending candle for Brighid with which to perform your flametending vigils. Next you will be introduced to an energy working that will open you up to Brighid's energy and facilitate deep communion with her. Then you will enter a guided meditation in which you will discover a special fire temple on the inner plane to visit when you are flametending. Lastly, when your outer and inner spaces have been readied, you will be guided to Brighid's Well of Wisdom to seek your quest for your first transformational flametending journey.

Ritual: Creating a Brighid-Flame Candle

If you are already flametending with a flametending order, you are likely already in possession of a Brighid-flame, a candle lit from the re-lit Brighid's Fire in Kildare. If you aren't yet a member of any flametending order, you can join one and tend the flame with them, and when you do, they will likely provide you with a Brighid-flame candle. However, if you don't wish to join an order and wish to begin flametending, you can dedicate your own Brighid-flame with the following ritual. If you are already in possession of a Brighid-flame candle, you can use this ritual to create a new one if you misplace yours.

Note that the Brighid-flame candle is the candle you will use to light the candles of the flame you will tend. The tradition of the Brighid-flame candle is that Brighid's essence and energy is retained in its wick, so each time it is used to light a new candle, her essence is passed into the new candle. Hence, you will always have a Brighid-flame from which to both light your tending candles and create new Brighid-flame candles for yourself when your first one runs low, or make Brighid-flames for others. You can use any candle that is easy for you to pick up and light other candles with; some use tea light candles, but I prefer short tapers.

After selecting your Brighid-flame candle, choose a candle you will light with it to tend Brighid's Fire. You can choose a tall taper, a pillar candle, a jar candle, or even a kerosene lamp with oil and a wick. I've used them all at one point or another; all can work well. Choose whatever works best for your particular space and needs, always with an eye to safety.

As this flametending practice is a daily practice, you will need a shrine for your Brighid-flame and tending candle. It need not be large, only big enough to hold these candles, a statue or image of Brighid, and a bowl in which to make offerings to her. Ensure the shrine won't be disturbed by children or pets, if those are relevant to you, that a candle or lamp can safely burn there, and that you can seat yourself comfortably before it during your flametending meditations.

This practice incorporates journaling, so also select a special journal for your flametending work. This can be as simple or as fancy as you like, from a composition notebook to an embossed, leatherbound blank journal, to something you fashion yourself if you are so talented and inclined. Keep your flametending journal on or near your Brighid shrine. You might also choose a special pen to write in it with, but this is not necessary.

Once you have gathered these items and arranged your shrine, you will be ready to create your Brighid-flame. Prepare a grain or dairy offering for Brighid before you begin the ritual, which could be bread, cake, pastry, milk, butter, or cheese, for example, and have it ready nearby. Combining these by offering buttered bread works well, too. Ensure that your offering will fit inside your offering bowl.

Begin the ritual by settling yourself before your shrine, then grounding and centering yourself with three deep breaths. Now make your offering to Brighid by placing it into the offering bowl on your shrine and recite this praise prayer to her, adapted from a medieval prayer to St. Brigit recorded by Gerald of Wales:

Victorious Brighid,
Glory of the gods,
Radiant Sun,
Noble lady,
Dangerous oath,
Perpetual Flame.
She holds the Torch,
Fostermother of the Gael,

Guide to flametenders,
Wisdom's spark,
Daughter of the Daghda,
Exalted One,
Victorious Brighid,
Life's living one.

Finish with another deep breath and feel Brighid's presence around your shrine for her, and her imbuing it with her energy. Now take up your Brighid-flame candle and matches or a lighter. Light the candle, then, to imbue it with Brighid's energy and essence, speak this adaptation of a traditional Scottish highland blessing over it:

I kindle my Brighid-flame this day/night
In the presence of holy Brighid —
The forge's fire of Brighid the Smith
Be within this candle,
The hearth's fire of Brighid the Healer
Be within this candle,
The imbas's fire of Brighid the Poet
Be within this candle,
The power of the Exalted One
Be within this candle,
Within its wick:
Within this candle,
Within its wick,
To be carried to all wicks it lights,
Each day and night,
Every day and night:
Each day and night,
Every day and night.
As it was, as it is, as it evermore shall be.

Let its flame grow for a moment, then use it to light the candle or lamp on your shrine where you will tend Brighid's Fire. As you do, recite this prayer adapted from an 11th century prayer to St. Brigit:

Brighid,
Excellent, Exalted One,
Bright, golden, quickening flame —
Shine your blessings on us from the Otherworld,
You,
Radiant fire of the sun.

Gently blow out your Brighid-flame candle and set it on your shrine, either in its own holder or sitting or lying down beside your tending candle. Sit with Brighid for a while and meditate with her as her Perpetual Fire now burns on your shrine for her. Ask her what she wants you to know right now about beginning this flametending journey in which you will tend her flame in the world while she teaches you how to tend your inner flame within. Pay attention to how she communicates with you; you may hear her voice speak, see images or words, perceive feelings or emotions, or receive thoughts or ideas.

When you feel your meditation has come to an end, finish it with words of praise: *All praises to Brighid.* Then take up your journal and record everything you felt, thought, and received from Brighid. When finished, gently extinguish your tending candle. You may dispose of your offerings outdoors or leave them on your shrine for three days, as is done in the Scottish tradition, to ensure that all the goodness from them has been extracted. You now have a Brighid-flame and a shrine on which to tend Brighid's Perpetual Fire.

Meditation: Journeying to Your Inner Fire Temple
This flametending practice is one of inner work, and so creating

an inner Fire Temple to visit when meditating helps facilitate this work. Doing this internal work then rounds out the physical flametending practice: as you tend Brighid's Fire on your shrine, you will simultaneously tend your spiritual fire within – and Brighid will be tending it with you. This is the key to the work: flametending is both a physical and a spiritual practice – as without, so within, and so within, so without. The outer fire is the torch that guides us within to the inner fire, where true transformation takes place.

Choose a time to perform this meditation when you will be undisturbed. Begin by making an offering to Brighid on your shrine, then light your flametending candle with your Brighid-flame as you recite the Flame Kindling prayer:

Brighid,
Excellent, Exalted One,
Bright, golden, quickening flame —
Shine your blessings on us from the Otherworld,
You,
Radiant fire of the sun.

Comfortably seat yourself upright, ground and center yourself with three deep breaths, and close your eyes. Open your inner vision to the following scene.

See yourself standing outside at twilight before the opening of a spiral path bordered on each side by tall evergreen hedges of yew. You carry a lantern to light your way as you walk the path toward your inner fire temple at the heart of the spiral. As you stand here, you become aware of the fire at the core of the earth beneath your feet. You inhale and breathe its energy up through your feet and legs into your pelvic area, where your Cauldron of Warming sits, your inner forge where your power of creation resonates with the earth's power of creation. Then you exhale and you feel this earth-fire energy brighten and grow within you. Now you take a step onto the spiral path and begin walking.

As you walk up the first arm of the first spiral to its top, you again breathe in the earth-fire, and when you reach the top of the first round of the spiral, you exhale slowly as you walk back down, feeling the earth-fire expand within your Cauldron of Warming. You proceed in this way until you have completed nine rounds of breath, walking around and around the spiral path. On your ninth exhalation, when you reach the spiral's ninth and final turn, you exit the path and see a small structure before you. Take note of what type of structure it is, what shape it is, what size it is, what materials it is built of. Take note, as well, of the grounds surrounding it, whether a wilderness of healing plants, a garden of medicinal herbs, a yard graced by an ancient oak tree, a healing well, a pool surrounded by hazel trees, or a furnished space for outdoor meditation. You are delighted with and comforted by the space you find and feel it was designed just for you.

When you have taken in your outdoor surroundings, you approach your fire temple's door and enter. As you step inside, you take some time to observe this space. Beside the door you notice a shelf and set down your lantern here. Nearby you see a rack and hang up the coat or cloak you were wearing outdoors. You notice Brighid's Fire burning in the very center of the room you are standing in and a hearth or shelf nearby upon which sit four pillar candles. A small basket sits on a low table or bench holding rush tapers for lighting them and a vase beside it with a bit of water in its bottom in which to extinguish the used tapers. A comfortable sitting space is set before Brighid's Fire for you to sit in and commune with Brighid. You take some time now to walk around your inner fire temple and observe what else is here, how it is designed and furnished, and what else the space invites you to do, whether herb work, crafting, writing, composing or playing music, or studying. In addition to your flametending meditations, you understand that you may visit your inner fire temple any other time you like for any other inner work overseen by Brighid.

When you have familiarized yourself with the space, you fetch your lantern and bring it over to the table or bench where the basket of tapers sits. You take up a taper, open the top or door of your lantern, and light the taper with the flame in the lantern. You close the lantern and take your taper to each pillar candle, lighting each in turn as you name the four faces of Brighid:

> *Brighid the Smith, Brighid the Healer, Brighid the Poet, Brighid the Dreamer.*

You then drop the taper down into the vase beside the basket to extinguish it. Standing before Brighid's Fire and the lit candles, you bless your inner fire temple by reciting this adaptation of a traditional Scottish highland house-blessing prayer:

> *Brighid,*
> *Excellent, Exalted One,*
> *Bless this temple*
> *From site to stay,*
> *From beam to wall,*
> *From end to end,*
> *From ridge to basement,*
> *From balk to roof-tree,*
> *From found to summit,*
> *Found and summit.*
> *As it was, as it is, as it evermore shall be.*
> *All praises to Brighid.*

You now settle yourself on your seating space before Brighid's Fire and become aware of how her fire sits at the heart of the temple and the temple sits at the heart of the spiral, just as the life-giving sun sits at the heart of Earth's never-ending journey around it. Observe that as the power of the sun feeds the earth around you, the power of Brighid's Fire feeds the light within you. You picture within you a crystalline heart, only this heart is not of a solid crystal, but a holographic one, glowing with multicolored lights. Just as you might set your own crystals outside in the sun to be charged by its energy, you breathe Brighid's Fire into this holographic crystalline heart within the energy center in your chest called the Cauldron of Motion, so Brighid may charge it with her energy. Just as when you walked the yew spiral, you take in her energy with each inhalation, and with each exhalation, feel her energy charge and fill your heart-space. As you do, you see and feel this holographic heart growing larger as it is filled and charged, until on your ninth and final exhalation, it has enlarged so that it reaches your Cauldron of Knowledge in your cranium and overturns it.

Once overturned, you exhale through the top of your head to send your vision upward where you picture a night sky of stars above you. The constellation of Cygnus, Brighid's Swan, stands out brightly, watching over and guiding you. You inhale and breathe her cosmic energy down through the top of your head and into your Cauldron of Knowledge, the energy center that resides behind your third eye. Its shining starfire fills and illuminates your inner cauldron, and as you exhale, you feel this energy expanding and filling it. You complete nine rounds of inhalations and exhalations, and feel Brighid's celestial light fill and surround you.

Now you sit and commune with Brighid for a while. You ask her what she wants you to know right now about being and working in your inner fire temple, paying attention to how she communicates with you.

When you feel you have received your messages from Brighid, you thank her for what she has imparted, then tell yourself, *I am ready to return.* With a deep breath in to bring Brighid's guidance with you, and a strong exhale through pursed lips to release the meditation, you bring yourself back to your physical body and home shrine. Slowly open your eyes, stretch yourself, and journal what you saw around and inside your inner fire temple and the information you received from Brighid. Set your offerings outdoors or do so three days later, as you prefer.

Return to your inner fire temple on the spiral path and perform these energy workings each time you flametend to strengthen your connection with Brighid so she can help you tend your inner flame, just as you tend her flame for her in the physical and spiritual realms.

Meditation: Visiting the Well of Wisdom

Now you are ready to seek your first quest from Brighid to work with through your first round of the twenty flametending vigils. This quest will be what you delve into over twenty successive days or nights with the guidance of Brighid to enact your transformative journey. Before you begin this meditation, ensure that you have your flametending journal and a pen nearby to record your experiences when the meditation is complete.

To begin, make an offering to Brighid, then light your tending candle with your Brighid-flame while reciting the Flame-kindling Prayer:

Brighid,
Excellent, Exalted One,
Bright, golden, quickening flame —
Shine your blessings on us from the Otherworld,
You,
Radiant fire of the sun.

Now settle yourself comfortably and close your eyes. Ground and center yourself with three deep breaths in and out, then open your inner sight to the following vision.

See yourself standing outside the entrance to the spiral path that leads to your inner Fire Temple. You are carrying a lit lantern in the dusk to light your way. You are excited because you are going to visit Brighid's Well of Wisdom to seek your inner quest. As you stand here, you become aware of the fire at the core of the earth beneath your feet. You inhale and breathe its energy up through your feet and legs into your pelvic area, where your Cauldron of Warming sits, your inner forge where your power of creation resonates with the earth's power of creation. Then you exhale and feel this earth-fire energy brighten and grow within you.

Now, instead of following the spiral path, you turn your back to it and observe a straight walking path extending to your left, which follows the path of a nearby river. This is the path to Brighid's Well of Wisdom. You step onto and begin following it.

As you walk, you inhale and again breathe up the energy of the earth's fiery core into your Caudron of Warming, then again exhale and feel it filling your pelvic area inside you. You follow this breathing pattern for nine breaths, and with each one, you quietly chant, "Brighid the Smith, guide my way."

Looking up, you see that the sun is riding close to the horizon, ready to set. You sense its rays reaching out to you and with your breath, you inhale and draw its energy into your heart center, where your Cauldron of Motion energy center sits, then exhale and feel the energy of this solar fire filling you. You follow this breathing pattern for nine breaths in total and at each one, you quietly chant, "Brighid the Healer, open my heart."

Now darkness has fallen and stars appear in the sky. You see Cygnus, Brighid's celestial swan, watching over and guiding you in the night. With an inhale, you breathe the energy of the starfire above down into you through the top of your head and into your energy center behind your third eye called the Cauldron of Knowledge. You see it warm and bright with your inner sight, and as you exhale, you feel it spread throughout your head, like a bright fire. You follow this breathing pattern eight more times to make nine altogether, and with each breath, you quietly chant, "Brighid the Poet, awaken my sight."

Upon completing these breaths, the path suddenly comes up to a ring of nine hazel trees. Before you enter this ring, to honor the sacred pool within, you make the traditional clockwise turn around the trees, reciting this prayer, a poem by Dennis King:

I walk sunwise
around standing stone,
well and sacred tree.
I walk sunwise
around mountain, lake
and wood.
I walk sunwise
on the path of the spiral
on the path of vision
on the path of truth.

Arriving back at the opening of the circle of trees where you began, you now enter and approach the Well of Wisdom. You seat yourself facing the water and then call on Brighid the Dreamer: "Brighid the Dreamer, please show me what I most need to know right now for my spiritual growth. Please give me a message showing me what I most need to focus on and work on inside myself at this time."

You still yourself, breathe steadily, and watch the waters of the well. Slowly, they begin to glow from beneath. Gradually, the light below grows brighter, until finally, a great flame breaches the water's surface and gently rises until it is hovering over the well. You focus on this flame and open yourself to what it shares with you, whether through words, thoughts, sounds, or visions dancing within it. Here you find the quest you seek – Brighid's Torch revealing what she will help you work on, what aspect of yourself would most benefit at this time from your attention. You sit intently taking in what she wishes to share with you. Then, however you received the information, you distill it into a word or two, like, for example, *compassion* or *creativity* or *self-love* or *abandonment*. This word becomes your quest and message to take forth onto your transformational flametending journey. You thank Brighid for her message and watch as the flame slowly sinks back into the well and down into its waters until its glow fades from sight.

With a deep breath, you see the scene before you fade, then feel yourself return to your body and space, and slowly open your eyes. Stretch your body, then record your quest in your journal and anything else you wish to recall about the experience. You will bring this quest with you to your first transformational flametending vigil. Gently extinguish your candle and set your offerings outdoors either now or three days later, as you prefer. Soon you will be ready to begin flametending!

Exercise: The Mantle of Brighid

The Mantle of Brighid is an energy exercise designed to help you open your energy to and commune with Brighid. It works with three internal energy centers the Irish tradition calls cauldrons, and which I correlate with Brighid the Smith, Brighid the Healer, and Brighid the Poet. These energy centers are detailed in the writing called The Cauldron of Poesy, designed to promote poetic inspiration. The energy you move will not only fill you, but surround you, as Brighid's protective and healing mantle is said to do. Use this exercise to prepare yourself for each meditation in your transformational flametending work.

To begin, welcome Brighid by lighting a candle to her with the Flame-kindling prayer:

Brighid,
Excellent, Exalted One,

Bright, golden, quickening flame —
Shine your blessings on us from the Otherworld,
You,
Radiant fire of the sun.

Then open the exercise by reciting the Rune of the Mantle of Brighid:

Brighid, you are
a bright star above me,
a smooth path before me,
a mantle of blessing about me,
and a crystalline heart within me.
As it was, as it is, as it shall ever be.

Now seat yourself comfortably, close your eyes and ground yourself with three deep breaths. In your mind's eye, picture your internal bone structure, and the three containers within you formed by your pelvic bones, ribcage, and skull.

In the first cauldron of the pelvic region, the Cauldron of Warming, envision a forge. Feel a connection in this region to the energy of the inner Earth, that roiling cauldron of liquid fire, and with your inhaling breath, draw that up into your Cauldron of Warming to light the fire of its forge. As you then exhale through pursed lips, feel and envision this forge fire igniting and intensifying. Take eight more rounds of these breaths to make nine in all, feeling this earth-fire energy grow within you as you inhale, and expand within you as you exhale. Now that the forge fire is burning hot and bright, envision yourself standing before it. With gloved hands, see yourself holding an iron item with tongs over its fire and striking it with a hammer until sparks fly upward. When they do, with your attention, follow the sparks upward inside you to your second inner cauldron in your chest. As you follow the sparks, take a deep breath in and draw the forge's hot energy into that second cauldron as well.

With your attention now in your heart center, picture a cauldron full of water hanging on a tripod over a fire pit where wood has been laid beneath it. See the sparks from the forge ignite the wood and watch the fire slowly build. As you inhale deeply, see the flames burning brighter, and as you exhale, feel the heat of the fire spread within your chest. Take eight more breaths in and out, seeing and feeling this fire grow. As it does, observe how the water in the cauldron warms, then boils. On your final round of breaths, notice that a low table stands beside the cauldron on which a bundle of herbs sits. Pick this up and place it into the cauldron. These herbs will help further open your inner sight. Now observe the steam rising from the boiling herbs, and with your attention, follow it up inside you into your third cauldron, inside your skull and behind your forehead. As you follow it, inhale deeply to bring the energy of the second cauldron up into the third, the Cauldron of Knowledge.

With your attention now on this third cauldron, in your mind's eye, picture a clear pool ringed by nine hazel trees. See the steam from the cauldron below rising up into its waters, rippling and energizing them. Slowly, a shimmering flame emerges from its depths until it hangs suspended over the pool, glowing like a beacon. As you inhale, feel this flame's energy intensify within your Cauldron of Knowledge, then feel it expand when you exhale. Breathe in and out through this cycle eight more times, to make nine in all. Once complete, on your next breath, return your focus to your first cauldron, to the forge.

Now with a deep inhalation, draw the energy of the forge right up through your other two cauldrons in a golden stream of light until it emerges from the top of your head, and then, with an exhalation through pursed lips, feel it fountain up and out, and cascade down all around your aura. Observe where any cracks or leaks may be in your energy field, and see this golden light filling them, creating a beautiful pattern with its golden seams. As the energy falls around you, gather it back into your Cauldron of Warming. Breathe this earth-fire energy up, through, and over you two more times, three times in all.

Now that your crown has been energetically opened, shift your focus back up to your third cauldron, the fire in the head. Sense the stars in the sky above you, and one in particular – Deneb, in the constellation of Cygnus the Swan. Brighid is connected with the swan in Scottish lore. Connect with the fiery glow of this star, then feel its light and heat falling down through the top of your head into your Cauldron of Knowledge, which is now upturned and ready to receive. Inhale this silvery, stellar energy and envision it pouring into your third cauldron. Observe how differently this stellar fire feels from the land's earth-fire energy, and as you exhale, fill the cauldron further. Follow this breathing cycle eight more times to make nine altogether, at which point, your Cauldron of Knowledge becomes filled to the brim and overflowing. As it spills over, with your attention, follow this energy downward as it lands in your now-upturned Cauldron of Motion in your heart center. Use your breathing in and out eight more times to completely fill this cauldron with the stellar energy flowing down into you from the cosmos. When your second cauldron is also filled, see how this one now overflows, and with your attention, follow this spillover down into your upturned Cauldron of Warming in your pelvic region. Take nine breaths again to fill up this cauldron. On your final breath, with a deep, full inhalation, pull this energy straight down from Cygnus's star, then, with a forceful exhalation, push this energy out the bottom of your spine and see it fountain up all around your aura in a silvery net, surrounding the golden layer from the earth-fire, protecting it with glittering light. As it balloons up and around you, feel it collect in your Caudron of Knowledge, where you then pull it down through you again with your breath and send it out, up, and around you once more. Finally, do this a third time, feeling the palpable bubble of energy around you and the protective boundary it creates to strengthen and hold the energy generated within it though activating your inner cauldrons.

Now shift your attention to your second cauldron in your heart center, the Cauldron of Motion. In your mind's eye, envision a clear, heart-shaped quartz crystal here, which is not only crystalline, but holographic – made of light. Connect this crystalline heart with the energy of Brighid's flame before you, then, with a deep breath in, draw Her energy into your holographic heart. Notice how this Brighid-fire energy differs in feel again from the stellar fire and earth fire. When you exhale, see and feel this energy intensifying and burning in the center of the crystalline heart, dancing in all the colors of the rainbow. Over the course of your next eight breaths, envision the energy of this holographic heart intensifying with each inhale and expanding with each exhale, growing larger, and filling with more Brighid-fire. See and feel this holographic heart as it first grows in size to fill your chest, then grows even larger as it surrounds your body, then finally expands further still to encompass your aura.

You are now sitting inside the Mantle of Brighid. Take three deep, slow breaths to simply rest inside this fortifying and nourishing energy generated from Brighid's three fires. Perform this exercise when you begin your first transformational flametending vigil, and thereafter on the first night of each new round of flametending vigils, to keep yourself open to Brighid and so her energies may continuously flow through you to nourish, strengthen, and protect you.

Chapter 4

The Ritual of the Flametending Vigil

The vigil is the time you spend in your daily flametending practice and each vigil is an opportunity to commune with Brighid to receive her guidance at each step of your journey. Schedule at least thirty minutes for each vigil to allow for the full experience of grounding, centering, journeying within, communing with Brighid, contemplating your prompt, and journaling your experience afterward to process it.

You can help build consistency in your practice by dedicating a specific time period each day to your flametending work. As with any contemplative practice, regularity is key to receiving the greatest benefit from it. Prepare for each vigil by reading through the pages in this book correlating with your current vigil's ogham tree and take in how the information offered therein leads you into another step toward transformation. This knowledge then ensures that you fully understand why you are performing the vigil. When you are then ready to begin, move through the following steps to perform the ritual of the flametending vigil.

Opening: Flame-kindling Prayer

Begin the flametending vigil by bringing yourself to full presence with three deep, slow breaths, then lighting your tending candle on your shrine while reading or reciting the Flame-kindling Prayer:

Brighid,
Excellent, Exalted One,
Bright, golden, quickening flame—
Shine your blessings on us from the Otherworld,

You,
Radiant fire of the sun.

First Vigil Only:
Offerings to Open the Journey's Way and Awakening the Cauldrons to Receive

Each time you begin a new cycle of the twenty flametending vigils, on its first vigil, make an offering to Brighid so she will open and light the way for your new journey. Traditionally, offerings of dairy and grain products are made to the Tuatha Dé Danann. Place a small plate or bowl with an offering of either or both products beside your image of Brighid on your shrine. After the vigil ends, discard it outdoors onto the earth, perhaps in an outdoor space you designate for this.

After you make your offering to Brighid and she opens the way, revitalize your inner cauldrons for the new journey's work by performing the Mantle of Brighid exercise. Not only does this energetic meditation awaken the inner cauldrons, it fortifies the energetic boundary of the aura, thereby creating a protected and sacred space for the body inside which to journey to and commune with Brighid. In the same way that we as flametenders tend the physical Perpetual Fire of Brighid on our personal shrines for her, so too do we tend the spiritual fire within our inner cauldrons, and both fires reflect and resonate with each other. And as we open our inner cauldrons to receive Brighid's energy, she then tends our inner flames as we tend her worldly flame.

For all of the other vigils, skip this step and proceed to the next one.

The Fire Temple Meditation

Perform the Inner Fire Temple Meditation to travel to your inner fire temple. This aligns the physical flame on your shrine with the cosmic flame in your fire temple so they may both feed your spiritual flame in your soul's sanctuary, which you can think of as an inner Cill Dara. There is no need to perform the temple blessing portion again though, as that is only done when you first enter it.

Communion

You have now aligned your physical, cosmic, and spiritual flames and opened your inner cauldrons, and are ready to receive Brighid's communion. In your meditation, visualize the Oak of Mugna expressing its current stage of development as described for each vigil outlined in the following chapter and contemplate how this stage of growth correlates with your quest. Commune silently with Brighid and take in any and all information she sends you, which may come via visions, voices, music, emotions, sensations, words, etc.

Returning

When you feel you have received all the information you are meant to, silently thank Brighid and close your meditation with three deep breaths. As you inhale, feel your attention move back into your body and the sensations of the surface beneath you, and as you exhale, see the fire temple around you fade away. Then slowly open your eyes and gently stretch to ground back into yourself.

Journaling

Respond to the Journal Prompt question in your flametending journal and record everything you received in your meditation. Let your flametending candle continue to burn if it is safe to do so and you would like to, or gently extinguish it in whatever manner feels best to you with the words, *All praises to Brighid.*

As you work through each vigil, you will see how each one builds upon the work of the past vigil and leads you into the work of the following one, and that each class similarly builds upon the previous class and leads into the one to follow. A story of your own transformation will begin to unfold over the course of the twenty vigils of the flametending cycle as you work ever more deeply with each quest you receive for each cycle's work. And then you will begin to also see how each new quest derives from the one previous, and will inform the one that will emerge from it. Just as a new candle can be lit from the guttering flame of a spent one, the flame of knowledge is revealed in each vigil, through each class and each quest, and passed along so that this fire remains forever lit and illumination can ever be offered.

Chapter 5

The Forest Path of the Flametending Journey
Your Quest with 20 Vigils & 20 Trees

Introduction to the Ogham Entries

The meanings associated with each ogham character stem from traditional lore attributed to each one. Primary information is derived from what are called word-oghams, poetic clues to each character's assigned spiritual meaning. These poetic clues, also called kennings, derive from three different lists, named *Word-Oghams of Morainn mac Móin*, *Word-Oghams of Maic ind Óc*, and *Word-Oghams of Con Culainn*. The first two are found in the Old Irish Ogam Tract, while the Con Culainn list derives from sixteenth and seventeenth-century manuscripts. In 1988, Damian McManus, a professor of Early Irish at Trinity College in Dublin, translated these word-oghams into English. Author and fellow flametender Erynn Rowan Laurie based her work in her book, *Ogam: Weaving Word Wisdom* (2007), in part on McManus's translations, and my work is largely based on hers. Per Laurie's system, I reference the source of the listed word-oghams as she does, with the abbreviations of MM for *Word-Oghams of Morainn mac Móin*, MO for *Word-Oghams of Maic ind Óc*, and CC for *Word-Oghams of Con Culainn*. Rather than list all three for each ogham character, I list the one that most resonates with how I work with the ogham in this flametending practice.

I also explore the word-ogham's deeper significance to this transformative flametending practice, offer a keyword derived from it, how the character's meaning fits into the process of its particular class, and a journal prompt to facilitate your inner work. I then associate each class with a face of Brighid and provide both a prayer to that aspect of her and a discussion of how this face guides the class's corresponding stage of your

43

inner transformation.

Through this turning cycle of growth, death, and rebirth, you can engender your inner development through consciously engaging with the energies present in your life and follow them through this arc as a form of gaining and deepening wisdom and insight about your spiritual self in the world.

And now, we step into the forest of ogham trees and tread the path of the transformational flametending journey. Each step is a vigil, marked by each tree in succession. As you move deeper into the forest, you more deeply affect your inner transformation by delving further into yourself as you commune with Brighid. And as you do, your soul gently moves through the stages of growing, fruiting, ripening, and seeding, as does the Oak of Mugna and its fruits of wisdom.

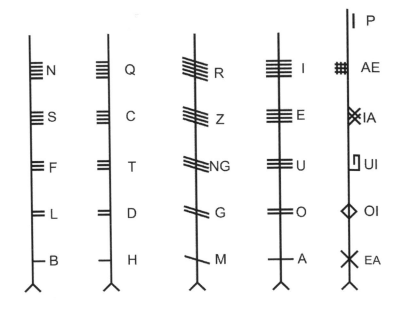

The Ogham alphabet.

Image used with permission from: https://commons.wikimedia.org/wiki/File:All_ Ogham_letters_including_Forfeda_-_%C3%9Cbersicht_aller_Ogham-Zeichen_ einschlie%C3%9Flich_Forfeda.jpg

Vigils 1-5: Growth
Class of Formation

The first five vigils of the flametending journey are represented by the first five ogham trees, which comprise the first class of the tree ogham. This class expresses the developmental stage of growth. The vigils begin with Beith, which speaks of newness and beginnings, like the season of spring. Viewing the seasons expressing through the growth stages of a tree, this segment of the ogham in this flametending practice corresponds to the life stages of a tree seed sprouting, the seedling growing, and the tree forming.

The silver bark and early catkins of the birch tree are most vibrant early in the year and the birch tree is associated in Scottish lore with Brighid, for whom a wand of birch was traditionally made on Brighid's Day to accompany a grain icon of her, so the birch is frequently associated in Gaelic culture with Imbolc, the Celtic celebration of spring on February 1st. In this first class of ogham trees on the flametending journey, the forms of both the Oak of Mugna and the current flametending cycle's quest take shape.

The lines of these tree characters are drawn horizontally to the right from a central vertical branch. The shape of these letters is suggestive of the steady growing of the mythic Oak of Mugna as it takes shape, and can be said to visually depict its stages of growth from seed to sapling to full-crowned tree. The descriptors of each tree on the following list combine meaning from each character's word-ogham with the stage of growth the tree takes in its progression of formation.

B: **Beith** – Birch – Initiation of Growth
L: **Luis** – Rowan – Luster of Sun that Feeds Growth
F: **Fearn** – Alder – Shape as Container for Growth
S: **Saille** – Willow – Sustenance of Water that Supports Growth
N: **Nion** – Ash – Peace Imparted by Grown Tree

Brighid the Smith resonates with and guides these steps of forming the planted reflection of the Cosmic Tree of Knowledge within you. When you have divined or determined your quest for the present flametending cycle, which could be *faith* or *sovereignty* or *discernment*, or anything at all, then you can engage with Brighid the Smith to guide your process of conscious creation and formation of the energy your quest entails. Brighid the Smith's purview is forming and shaping, and just as she forms raw metal into practical and beautiful tools and weapons, so she assists in spiritual formation as you construct the supportive spiritual container for your inner work in the form of an inner Tree of Life. One of the three fruits said to grow on the Oak of Mugna is acorns. It is often said that from tiny acorns mighty oaks grow, and indeed, from the seed of your spiritual quest, a powerful container of spirit is formed to collect the wisdom you will gain along the quest of your flametending journey.

As the Oak of Mugna grows into its form, Brighid the Smith guides you in shaping a solid foundation for your inner work which will in turn feed the growth of your inner soul sanctuary, which you can think of as your inner Cill Dara, that contains and protects your spiritual energy as it grows in power through your flametending work.

When you begin your first flametending vigil, hold your hand over your Cauldron of Warming, your inner seat of Brighid's forge, and recite this prayer to Brighid the Smith to open the work of the Class of Formation:

Brighid of Power, Life's Living One, Creator, Forger, and Shaper, walk with me through this class and teach me to shape my path and my understanding of myself. As you grow the seed into the mighty oak tree, show me how to forge the tools I need to grow in wisdom and strength to wholeness. As it was, as it is, as it evermore shall be.

Vigil 1: Beith – Birch
Keyword: Initiation

Rather than taking this tree's keyword and meaning from any of the word-oghams associated with it, I take this one from the mythic creation of the Tree Ogham itself. In the Irish tradition, the god Ogma is said to have carved this character seven times on a twig to both warn and protect the god Lugh's wife, as she was being pursued by fae folk intending to kidnap her. This mythic act initiated the ogham alphabet itself, and so it serves here as an initiator of your flametending journeys, as well as of Brighid's guidance and protection as you proceed.

In this first step of the journey, your initial message from Brighid at the Well of Wisdom, or the seed of your new quest from your subsequent journey, symbolically emerges from underground to begin its formation.

During your meditation, visualize this seed's first thin stem and seed-leaves breaching the boundary of the underworld and unfurling in fresh air. As you see this new growth appearing, commune with Brighid and ask her to reveal to you what will be most helpful for you to know about this cycle's quest as you begin your journey with it. Remain in your meditation with her for as long as needed to receive what she wants you to know. When you have received her guidance, close your meditation, open your eyes, and journal your response to the following prompt.

Journal Prompt: *What does Brighid want me to know right now about this quest?*

Vigil 2: Luis – Rowan
Keyword: Luster
Word-ogham: *lí súla* – luster of eye (MM)

Luster is a shine of light, like fire, which reminds of the Perpetual

47

Fire of Brighid. It also reminds of the sun, the great fire that lights our world. Light is needed for growth. As the fire and light of the sun feed the growing seedling of the mythic Oak of Mugna, the spiritual light of Brighid's Eternal Fire feeds our soul tree, Cill Dara, and fuels our spiritual growth.

In this vigil's meditation, visualize the seedling that has broken out of the darkness now reaching upward for the light and as you do, contemplate what light you reach toward that will fuel your own spiritual growth at this time. That which will feed your growth will help form the meaning of your quest and your journey toward fulfilling it.

Journal prompt: *How can the meaning of this quest encourage me to grow?*

Vigil 3: Fearn – Alder
Keyword: Container
Word-ogham: *comet lachta* – container of milk, i.e. a bowl (MO)

When you break a stem of dandelion, its milk is released. When you cut a branch from a tree, its sap runs. The tree is a container of power and life force, as is your body; your body will also bleed, or release its life force, if cut. Now that the Oak of Mugna is taking in the food of light, it is strengthening its container of life force. Similarly, as your soul has begun taking in spiritual food from Brighid's Eternal Fire, your soul tree, Cill Dara, is simultaneously beginning to grow in power. A strong container is better able to hold the power of life force than is a weak container, and as you strengthen your spiritual container with this work, you begin to become more able to contain and embody life force, which is spiritual power, which can then be directed toward affecting your transformation.

In this meditation, visualize the seedling becoming a sapling, branching out into the world and unfurling more leaves to take in more light to fuel more growth and build its strength, and simultaneously feel the power of Cill Dara strengthening within you. Contemplate what in your current quest needs to be held within your strengthening spiritual container and how you can embody it in your daily life moving forward through this cycle's journey.

Journal Prompt: *How can I embody the meaning of this quest?*

Vigil 4: Saille – Willow
Keyword: Sustenance
Word-ogham: *lúth bech* – sustenance of bees (MO)

Just as the growing Oak of Mugna reaches upward to the light for food, its roots must reach down to find water for sustenance to fuel its growth. No living thing can grow without water. Water reminds of Brighid's healing wells whose waters provide sustenance to ailing bodies so they may recover their health and wholeness. Where the branches of the Oak of Mugna reach up toward the light of the sun, its roots travel downward in the dark to seek the nourishment of moisture, seeking what is needed by sense rather than sight, just as wells bring water up from blind depths.

In this meditation, visualize strong roots in the dark beneath the earth lengthening and reaching for the nourishing water table below to help grow its form. As the Oak of Mugna's roots reach down into mythic soil for cosmic waters, so do Cill Dara's roots reach down into the unseen for what your current quest is indicating that you most need now for spiritual sustenance. You cannot see what it is, but Brighid will show you and lead you there. When you find it, bring it with you into your daily life to nourish yourself in whatever ways you are guided to do so.

Journal Prompt: *How does the meaning of this quest nourish me?*

Vigil 5: Nion – Ash

Keyword: Peace

Word-ogham: *costud side* – establishing of peace (MM)

Of the five mythic guardian trees of the five Irish provinces, of which the Oak of Mugna is one, three of them are ash trees. Therefore, the ash has strong connections to the concept of the World Tree, and the nearby Norse people envisioned their world tree as an ash. When the world or guardian tree stands strong, all the world, both seen and unseen, is in proper balance. Both the Oak of Mugna and Cill Dara can stand tall when they are equally fed by the twin powers of cosmic light and chthonic moisture that strengthen their form and nourish their vitality.

Now that you have engaged in the spiritual work of feeding your soul with spiritual light and nourishing it with spiritual waters to strengthen its form and the power it contains, the inner of tree of Cill Dara has fully grown within you, as the Oak of Mugna has done in its mythic realm. Visualize both the mythic and spiritual trees standing tall and strong, and feel that all is right within you and around you as the cosmos mirror and support your growth. Your inner and outer forms are in balance, and balance brings peace. Rest in and contemplate the peace your current quest brings to your life and how you can engage with it daily to maintain your balance.

Journal Prompt: *How does the meaning of this quest create peace for me?*

Vigils 6-10: Fruiting
Class of Examination

In this second class of ogham trees in the flametending journey, the quest of the flametending cycle becomes evident as the Oak of Mugna blooms and sets fruit, thereby activating the development of the created form's intended purpose, which is always ultimately to become whole. The opening of its buds can symbolize courage, as it takes courage to be vulnerable in order to bloom into our wholeness as we become who we truly are. In this class, you come into wholeness by examining and working through the fears embedded in your journey's quest. Through doing so, you will experience healing, which will release the energy that was locked in your fear to help you bloom and grow more fully into your potential. And this process will transform and strengthen your spirit.

The second class begins with hÚath, Hawthorn, whose blooming traditionally heralds the arrival of the Irish summer season at the feast of Bealtaine on May 1st, so handily demonstrates the next seasonal development of our tree: its summertime flowering, pollinating, and fruiting.

These characters are written by drawing lines horizontally to the left from the central vertical branch. This can be taken to signify inner balancing and growth toward realizing your quest's meaning and purpose after the outward growth of form in the previous class of vigils. This inner focus also feeds the development of the inner soul sanctuary, Cill Dara.

H: **hÚath** – Hawthorn – Naming the Fear
D: **Dair** – Oak – Rising Above and Overcoming Fear
T: **Tinne** – Holly– Protection Against Fear
C: **Coll** – Hazel – Wisdom Leading to Wholeness
Q: **Quert** – Apple – Power of Realized Wholeness

Brighid the Healer resonates with the second ogham class's work of finding nourishment and strength in what the previous stage of spiritual formation produced. Just as all parts of a plant or tree might be used, if amenable, for food or medicine, including the bitter parts, what this Tree of Life produces spiritually nourishes and strengthens us, bitterness and all. All life seeks balance through constant calibration; when our bodies are dis-eased and unwell, they crave and seek the means and materials necessary to recover ease and wellness. Brighid the Healer is the master of this process.

In this class, as you delve into and examine what is dis-eased and unwell within the relevant and immediate energy of your quest, Brighid the Healer guides you in exploring what ease and wellness might mean you us in this context, and how you can calibrate your inner self to align with it.

This second ogham class ends with Quert, or Apple. Apple is both one of the fruits said to grow on the Oak of Mugna and the namesake of one of the isles of the mythic Irish Otherworld – the Isle of Apples. In a medieval Irish tale called The Voyage of Bran, this island is said to be "without grief, without sorrow, without death, without any sickness, without debility, that is the sign of Emain--uncommon is an equal marvel." *Emain* refers to *Emain Abhlach*, which is what the Isle of Apples is called in Irish. Your work in this class will therefore lead you to the knowledge of how to relieve the dis-ease within you that is impeding your quest. By examining and retrieving this energy, your soul will gain more resources to apply to its journey toward wholeness.

The fruit of spiritual examination heals inner dis-ease by returning the soul to balance, which cultivates spiritual wholeness. Brighid the Healer can guide and support this work. As the Healer restores and rebalances vital energy in the body, so the vitality of the Oak of Mugna channels its vitality into blooming, pollinating, then setting fruit to produce the tree's intended purpose – to bring wisdom to the world to restore and rebalance humanity.

The work of this class strengthens the inner spirit and its manifestation in this practice as Cill Dara, the soul's inner sanctuary. Note that during this class of fruiting, all three fruits of the Oak of Mugna are represented and set: acorns with Dair/Oak, hazelnuts with Coll/Hazel, and apples with Quert/Apple. Each is associated with wisdom in the Irish tradition.

When you are ready to begin your vigil on Night Six, hold your hand over your Cauldron of Motion, the inner seat of Brighid's hearth fire and cauldron of healing at your heart center, as you recite this prayer to Brighid the Healer to open the work of the Class of Examination:

Brighid the Healer, I call on you to walk with me through this ogham class to help me face and heal my fear. Teach me how to heal myself so that your power to make the broken whole becomes my power as well. As it was, as it is, as it evermore shall be.

Vigil 6: hÚath – Hawthorn

Keyword: Fear
Word-ogham: *ansam aidche* – most difficult at night (CC)

What keeps us up at night are our anxieties and fears. They also arrest our development, spiritual and otherwise, which prevents us from blossoming into all we could be. Our fears keep us inside ourselves, in our comfort zones. Breaking out of them is difficult and risky, but must be done if we are to become all we can and are meant to be.

In this second class of the tree ogham, the fully grown Tree of Knowledge that is the Oak of Mugna is setting buds to begin its process of fulfilling its purpose – to produce the fruit of wisdom. The inner spiritual tree of Cill Dara does the same, but will not bloom if held back by fear. Spiritual growth is stunted by refusing to face and name fears, but can proceed when fear is learned from and overcome.

In your meditation, visualize the Oak of Mugna setting bud. As you do so, ask Brighid to help you take your first step toward recognizing and naming a fear you hold inside and around this journey's quest that has held you back from blossoming in your spiritual growth. Then consider what you and your life would look like were that fear to be completely healed.

Journal Prompt: *What fear do I hold around this quest that needs healing, and how would I be transformed were it healed?*

Vigil 7: Dair – Oak
Keyword: Strength
Word-ogham: *ardam dosae* – most exalted tree (MM)

Dair is the most exalted tree of the tree ogham due to both the strength of the oak's wood and the spiritual power of wisdom it conveys as the tree embodying druidic wisdom. Channeling this strength will help you overcome the fear that has arrested your spiritual development. Just as your journey's quest holds the fear that keeps you from blossoming, it also holds the key to healing and overcoming that fear so you can bloom into the image of how you visualized yourself as healed in your last meditation.

In this meditation, ask Brighid to help you see into your quest to find what in it can bring you the healing that will allow you to overcome your fear. When you know, feel the release of fear's grip on you and visualize the buds on the Oak of Mugna relaxing and opening into the sun. As you put into practice in your daily life what you are shown in this mediation, you will bring yourself closer to wholeness and strengthen your spiritual sanctuary that is Cill Dara.

Journal Prompt: *How does this quest help me overcome my fear?*

Vigil 8: Tinne – Holly
Keyword: Protection
Word-ogham: *smuir gúaile* – fires of coal, i.e. iron, marrow of charcoal, i.e. molten ingot (MM)

Just as medicine can be curative by healing illness, it can also be preventative by preserving and protecting health. Tinne's word-ogham speaks to iron, which is forged into tools and weaponry.

Preventative medicine is like a weapon against dis-ease, whether the dis-ease is physical, mental, emotional, or spiritual, and all the overlap among them that is usually present.

Iron is also used in the Irish tradition to protect against the malignant intentions of the fae folk by either carrying a small piece, or ingot, in a pocket or setting an ingot on a windowsill to protect home and family from misfortune. Just as iron is used in these ways for protection, Tinne can be used here as protection from fear that holds you back from growing, from fully developing into wholeness. When the buds of the tree are protected, they are able to open in full bloom so they can fulfill their purpose by pollinating to set fruit, the fruits of wisdom on the Oak of Mugna, the cosmic Tree of Knowledge.

A powerful tool to employ to protect against the destructive energy of fear is a sigil, a meaningful symbol imbued with protective power. This quest you are working with shows you many things: how you can grow, what the fear that is that's holding you back from growing, how you can overcome that fear, and also how it offers protection from this fear.

During this meditation with Tinne, ask Brighid to show you a symbol that will protect you from the arresting energy of fear so it cannot interfere with your spiritual growth on your journey. When you see it, draw it on your palms and over your inner cauldrons with your finger to protect your energy so it can safely move you into your next stage of development.

After you have drawn your sigils into your energy, visualize the flowers adorning the Oak of Mugna showering their pollen over the tree in a golden light. Sit inside this light and feel it enter into your spiritual center, your Cill Dara, and know that wisdom will soon come to you from this pollination of cosmic and spiritual energies. Be sure to record your sigil into your journal after, as this is now a powerful tool you may utilize whenever you feel it is needed.

Journal Prompt: *How does the meaning in this quest protect me from this fear?*

Vigil 9: Coll – Hazel
Keyword: Wisdom
Word-ogham: *carae blóesc* – friend of cracking, friend of nutshells (MO)

Hazel trees and nuts are renown in Irish tradition as symbols of wisdom. Nine hazel trees ring the mythical Well of Knowledge, into which their nuts fall and stain its waters red and purple. Red is the color of otherworldly influence in the Irish tradition. This well also holds the legendary salmon of wisdom, who attained wisdom from eating the nuts that fell into the well, and whose scaly skin is bedecked with the red stains and speckles of the Otherworld and its mystical knowledge.

In the safe space created through protection, your spirit fully opened within you so pollination could take place between the greater cosmic energies and your inner spiritual energies to further reveal to you the meaning and purpose of your journey's quest. Healing your fear allowed your spirit to bloom. After the flowers of the Oak of Mugna are pollinated, fruit begins to set – the fruit of wisdom that will grow into its fullness, just as you will glean deeper understanding of your inner journey to bring you closer to wholeness.

In your meditation, visualize the Oak of Mugna's flower petals pulling back and falling away to reveal the beginnings of hazelnuts, acorns, and apples growing in their place, taking shape and filling with the cosmic tree's energies. Breathe those energies into yourself, into your soul sanctuary, your Cill Dara within, where spiritual fruit of wisdom is also setting, and ask Brighid to show you what the meaning of your quest reveals about attaining wholeness, and what that wholeness looks and feels like. Spend time opening up to this response, as the wisdom it imparts is your blueprint to follow for the remainder of your journey with this quest.

Journal Prompt: *How can the meaning in this quest lead me to wholeness and what does that wholeness look and feel like?*

Vigil 10: Quert – Apple

Keyword: Empowerment

Word-ogham: *Brig anduini* – force of a man, substance of an insignificant person (MO)

In the Irish tradition, apples are magical keys to the Otherworld – branches of golden or silver apples are shaken to release a musical sound that transports the holder of the branch through the mists separating the worlds into the mythic realm of creation from where everything of this world originates, and where the gods can be met. Apple branches of bronze, silver, and gold were carried by traditional poets as signs of their office, and the apple branch is a symbol of those wise ones who know the power of life and death – the druids. The apple branch is powerful.

The first word in the word-ogham for Quert is *brig*, or *brígh*, which means substance, pith, or power. It is also the stem of Brighid's own name: The Exalted One, the one of exalted power, the powerful one. With her guidance in facing and overcoming your fear and opening to knowledge and wisdom, you become empowered – the opposite of an *anduini*, an insignificant person, or one who lacks power. With the apple branch, you can embody the power of Brighid's creative force to help you along your journey of transformation, thus able to receive, be changed by, and grow from what your quest wants you to experience and learn so you can evolve into wholeness. The power of the apple branch elevates us from spiritually bereft to spiritually full and whole.

Likewise, the Oak of Mugna's set fruit now swells to its own fullness, full of cosmic knowledge. With the apple branch, the wisdom in the quest empowers you, and this power then enables you to cross from the second class of the tree ogham to the third, where the fruit of wisdom ripens and you will be able to ingest and integrate what it has to teach you.

In your meditation, visualize both the cosmic Oak of Mugna and your inner Cill Dara, both covered with their fruits of wisdom. Then, like shaking the apple branch to part the mists and reveal the hidden Otherworld, ask Brighid to reveal to you the hidden meaning of your quest that you haven't yet discerned, that lies on the other side of your everyday understanding. When this hidden meaning is revealed, its energy will become available to you and empower your soul. It will also empower your intuition, to help you better discern subtle messages from the spirit realms, which will aid you in the next ogham class, with its work of illumination. Be sure to record everything in your flametending journal after your meditation concludes.

Journal Prompt: *How does the hidden meaning of my quest empower me?*

Vigils 11-15: Ripening
Class of Illumination

The fruits of wisdom on the Oak of Mugna, the mythic Tree of Knowledge, are now fully formed and ready to ripen, to process its internal pith into sweetness ready for ingesting. And with the eating of these cosmic fruits, we internally receive and process the message's cosmic knowledge so that it may yield spiritual illumination and transform us through deeper understanding.

The third class begins with *Muin*, Vine, which might be conceived of as grape or blackberry vines, suggesting the season of harvest, which is marked by Lughnasadh, the Irish celebration harvest and autumn on August 1st. In this class or season, the purpose of our tree's growth culminates in the colorful and sweet ripening of the Oak of Mugna's fruit of wisdom, ready to be consumed.

Just as processing ripe fruit into jams and jellies is work, so in this third ogham class you will be doing the work of processing the wisdom and power you gleaned in your meditations during the second class into tangible tools you can use for yourself even beyond this journey, to continue your learning and illuminate your life's spiritual journey. This work will be revealed in each vigil's description. The themes of each of these ogham trees will be like an arsenal of powerful potions lining your magical cabinet, ready to use to illuminate what still remains hidden.

The characters of the third class of ogham trees now feature branch lines drawn fully across their central trunks, from left to right, equally extended on each side. However, they are drawn diagonally, from top left to bottom right. We can perceive these slanted branches as resembling a tree's branches weighed down with ripened fruit ready for harvesting. This third class represents the season of harvest as the tree's fruits come ripe and the Oak of Mugna completes its growth cycle. The fruits of the Tree of Knowledge are ready to be consumed.

M: **Muin** – Vine – Illumination Through Voice
G: **Gort** – Ivy – Illumination Through Satisfaction
NG: **nGétal** – Broom – Illumination Through a Healing Charm
S: **Straif** – Blackthorn – Illumination Through a Mystery Revealed
R: **Ruis**: Elder – Illumination Through Channeling Intensity

After the examination and healing processes of the previous class, we enter the second half of the ogham with the third class representing ripening, as the formation and examination work now crystalizes into ripened wisdom that offers illumination. Just as the fruit on the Tree of Life ripens into sweet and edible form, so can the insight gained from formation and examination now be metabolized within you into words and forms which can speak to and empower your deeper, subconscious self.

Where the first half of the ogham shows us our inner microcosm, the second half shows us the macrocosm of which we are a part, and most importantly, how the world within reflects the world without, and as we tend our inner spiritual flame, the greater Perpetual Fire of the Universe in turn tends and enlivens us. Brighid the Poet can guide and support this process, with which she resonates.

Poets distill deep insights and powerful knowledge into poetry – that language of the numinous – to share cosmic and spiritual wisdom with others. Brighid is said to have been primarily worshipped as a divine poet, especially by poets. She is the one called on to bring imbas, or poetic inspiration, that creative spark borne from the friction of rubbing our personal emotions onto the larger cosmic forces that contain and illuminate them. The poet then speaks that illumination, called the fire in the head, into words of power

In this third ogham class, you will draw upon the tools of the poet to engage in processing work that will lead to illumination from your experiences with examining, overcoming, and healing your fear. That work empowered you to be ready for this process of transforming your pain into wisdom, both personal and cosmic, which will further fortify your inner soul sanctuary, Cill Dara.

When you are ready to open the third stage of the transformational flametending journey, hold your hand over your Cauldron of Knowledge, Brighid's inner seat of the flame of imbas over the Well of Wisdom, and recite this prayer to Brighid the Poet to open the way to your work with the Class of Illumination:

Brighid the Poet, I call on you to walk with me through this third class of the tree ogham help me transmute my words of fear into

words of power. Teach me to speak my true self into being and stand in my power as the creator of my world, both inner and outer, and align myself with the cosmic powers that move all of creation, so that your power to speak worlds into being becomes my own. As it was, as it is, as it evermore shall be.

Vigil 11: Muin – Vine
Keyword: Voice
Word-ogham: *conar gotha* – path of the voice (CC)

Opening the Class of Ripening is Muin, the vine weighed down with the ripe fruits of wisdom to harvest and ingest. Poets speak words of wisdom after communing with the cosmic power of the divine, translating that power into words conveying universal mystery to everyone. The poet is the conduit from the cosmic to the earthly realm, speaking the voice of the cosmos carried in the mythic Oak of Mugna to our inner soul sanctuaries, Cill Dara. It is the spirit that hears and knows the wisdom being revealed. In this Class of Ripening, everything in this soul journey will come together to illuminate the full meaning and power of your quest.

During this meditation, visualize the Oak Mugna heavy with the ripe fruits of acorns, apples, and hazelnuts, radiating the fullness of the great tree was intended to express. Feel that energy radiating into your soul sanctuary, your inner Cill Dara, empowering it to greater and deeper understanding and insight.

As you visualize the Oak of Mugna and feel its energy, recall the hidden meaning in your quest that Brighid revealed to you in your last meditation. Then, ask Brighid for imbas, or poetic inspiration, to transform that hidden meaning into words of power in the form of a poetic affirmation of this power to speak to yourself daily to fortify your soul.

Don't worry if you feel you aren't a poet or a writer – trust that Brighid will guide you to the words you need at this time. A poem can comprise just one word or two; your affirmation need not be elaborate, or rhyme, or adhere to any poetic structure. It is a poem because the goddess of poetry gave it to you, and only you, for this express, sacred purpose of empowering your spirit. Accept this illumination with gratitude and use it daily to fortify your soul. Words have greater power when spoken aloud and this is why historically, poetry is an oral tradition, because our voices charge the written word with the force of our emotions. Connect with the power of this affirmation when you speak these words aloud to yourself to bring that hidden power fully into this world.

Remember too to record it in your flametending journal afterward. Copy it onto something you will see daily and set it where you will remember to speak it to yourself, perhaps on your Brighid shrine or near a mirror. Feel the power of these words each day as you speak them aloud. Use this affirmation daily until your next quest reveals a new affirmation for you.

Journal Prompt: *What poetic affirmation does the hidden meaning and power of my quest reveal?*

Vigil 12: Gort – Ivy
Keyword: Satisfaction
Word-ogham: *sásad ile* – sating or satisfaction of multitudes (CC)

Ingestion of the fruit of knowledge brings satisfaction to the search for wisdom, whose revelation is illumination, which fills the soul sanctuary with the light of understanding and insight. Light is brought to where once was darkness, and what was hidden can now be seen.

In your meditation, visualize yourself sitting beneath the Oak of Mugna, where you are plucking and tasting of its fruits. Their wisdom then lights you up from within. As your inner sight is further opened, ask Brighid the Poet to show you a symbol that encapsulates the essence of your quest fully actualized, fully formed, blossomed, and ripened in its complete meaning and power. Sit with her until your inner sight can clearly see this symbolic image in all its fullness – all its angles, colors, and dimensions – and your spirit can both fully feel the energy it contains and understand what it means for you. When you have the fullness of it, in every sense, bring it into your soul sanctuary, your Cill Dara, where it can continue to illuminate and fortify your spirit with its energy.

Record your symbolic image in your flametending journal, along with everything it means. Soon afterward, find a way to physically create the image real by either drawing or painting it, fashioning it out of something, or purchasing an item resembling or depicting it. Keep it on your Brighid shrine until the next image of the next cycle is revealed, so its energy in the physical world can resonate with the energy of it in your soul sanctuary, to further align you with its energy and illumine your way.

Journal Prompt: *What symbolic form does my fully actualized quest take?*

Vigil 13: nGétal – Broom
Keyword: Healing Charm
Word-ogham: *lúth lego* – a physician's strength and cry (MM)

The physician's strength is to make whole what is broken, to heal disease into ease. In the Irish and Scottish traditions, reciting healing charms was often done as part of the physician's healing work. Both Brighid the Poet and Brighid the Healer understand the powers of voice and words and readily employ them to great effect through the use of charms.

Now that the quest's full meaning has been revealed, it can do what it was intended to – transform you. Spiritual transformation is a healing process by way of creating wholeness. The energetic symbol of the quest is stored within your soul's sanctuary, your inner Cill Dara, and from there, both its energy and illuminated meaning will work to heal you from the inside out. The symbol's energy is the macrocosmic energy carried within the cultural code of the symbol, while the deep meaning of the quest is the microcosmic application of that energy to your specific circumstance. When these two come into alignment, all your pieces are brought back together into a harmonious whole, which transforms you in that moment from fractured to healed. Healing is whole-ing, and whole-ing is healing; they are one and the same. And realigning with wholeness is always transformative.

In your meditation, connect with and feel your quest's symbol within your soul sanctuary, and as you focus your feeling on it, also focus your mind on the revealed meaning of your message. You could also hold your drawing or image of the symbol as you do this. As your focus allows the cosmic energy of the symbol to align with the personal energy of the quest, feel them merge within you and their edges sublimate into one great light of illumination. Sit in this light and let it fill every cell and pore of your physical and energetic being and sense how the alignment of this light is bringing all your fractured pieces to wholeness in this moment, and notice how this wholeness feels. Ask Brighid to gift you the words of a healing charm which carry the energy of this wholeness. Stay with her until you see, hear, or sense them, then recite them three times so your voice can further empower this energy of transformation.

When your meditation ends, record your healing charm into your flametending journal and recite it daily until you receive your next healing charm in your next journey so it can strengthen your transformation by reminding you of the energy of alignment and wholeness you experienced in your meditation.

Journal Prompt: *What healing charm can I write and recite to maintain the power of this transformative energy within me?*

Vigil 14: Straif – Blackthorn
Keyword: Mystery Revealed
Word-ogham: *mórad rún* – increase of secrets (MO)

The word-ogham for straif – *increase of secrets* – carries within it the inferred understanding that great secrets carry great meaning, and by learning how to see those secrets, the knowledge and mystery hidden within them can be revealed. A previously unseen truth comes to light.

The gaining of wisdom and understanding is not quite the end of any journey, for once wisdom is obtained and brings us into wholeness, that wholeness itself transforms us; we are suddenly no longer what we were before. One secret is that we were always whole, as spirit always is, but we were not experiencing wholeness. What transforms us is both our experience of feeling whole and what we then perceive from that experience of wholeness. What was hidden as a secret that we were unable to perceive from our unhealed experience is suddenly made visible to our healed selves – a great mystery is revealed.

Your quest has more to reveal to you. Now that you have aligned with and experienced wholeness, you and your perception have been transformed. You are now seeing cosmically as well as personally; mythically as well as concretely – you are now experiencing and viewing the world as the poet does: multidimensionally. The torch of Brighid broadens your vision and understanding so that you can appreciate the entire breadth and depth of the fullness of your quest, to not only now see it, but feel the gravity of its truth. Truth is what keeps us aligned with the cosmos so that we can then walk in spiritual integrity and maintain our state of wholeness, including our awareness of it.

In your meditation, visualize yourself seated beside Brighid's Well of Wisdom at dusk. As the sun sets, a light from beneath the water slowly rises to the surface, and as soon as the sun dips below the horizon, this light breaches the confines of the well and floats above it. This is Brighid's torch of imbas. As you look upon it, feel it brightly shining into your Cauldron of Knowledge and awakening your inner sight, the soul's eye that sees the hidden mysteries. Now look back down into the well. Where you just moments ago only saw water, you now see something else playing out across its surface. You may see images, words, symbols, or the waters themselves may behave in unusual ways. Pay close attention to whatever you see, for this is your quest's mystery being revealed to you, a previously unseen truth that will carry your understanding even deeper into your soul. Sit with it until you see, feel, and understand it clearly. This will show you how to walk in truth and maintain your newfound wholeness. Afterward, record everything you have seen in your flametending journal.

Journal Prompt: *What previously unseen truth does my quest now reveal in my wholeness?*

Vigil 15: Ruis – Elder
Keyword: Channeling Intensity
Word-ogham: *tindem rucci* – most painful of shames, most intense blushing (MM)

As the Cauldron of Poesy denotes, poetic inspiration comes when the Cauldron of Motion in the heart center is activated by emotion and the power of such intense feelings as pain, sadness, anger, and shame, as well as love, joy, and ecstasy. As their intensity builds, their emotional energies rise within and overturn the Cauldron of Knowledge so it can then receive imbas, the poetic "fire in the head" of inspiration. Once filled with imbas, the emotional energies are transmuted into poetic speech. Fully opening the heart to everything that must be felt is part of the poet's process of practicing this transformational art of composing poetry.

Revealed truths, like the one you discovered in your last meditation, also tend to reveal intense emotions. Old wounds are healed by such truths, but only after once again considering and experiencing past pain. The purpose of pain is to capture our attention so we might gain important insights.

When you have perceived the lesson it has for you, you can then transform energies like rage and shame by channeling them into exploring where your passions lie and what would kindle them to bring you joy. Let your recovered wholeness and transmuted energies launch you into the wonder of fresh, new experiences! Then feel these passionate and joyful energies fill and permeate the spaces of your inner sanctuary, your Cill Dara within. These will be the fuel that will warm and power you through the winter of the journey to come. From this place, you will then be ready to enter the final leg of your quest and ogham journey.

In this meditation, envision yourself seated beneath the great Oak of Mugna, heavy with its fruits of wisdom. Ask Brighid the Poet to help you see any pain that may lie inside the truth that was recently revealed to you. Consider what it wants to teach you. Ask it to illuminate its lessons for you. Now, from your vantage place of wholeness, ask Brighid to help you see how you can channel the energy of this pain into passion and joy, to bring the wholeness inside you to your daily living. Your Cauldron of Knowledge is ready to receive her inspiration! When you have it, close your meditation with thanks and record everything in your flametending journal. Then set about putting that inspiration into action!

Journal Prompt: *What does my pain want to teach me? And now that I have gained insight from it, what passions and joys do I now feel called to pursue and express?*

Vigils 16-20: Seeding
Class of Transformation

The fruit of wisdom on the Oak of Mugna, the Tree of Knowledge, has been tasted and ingested, and has elicited its illumination. Now that it has served its purpose, it withers on the branch as it prepares to fulfill its destiny: to die and be reborn.

The fourth class of the tree ogham opens with *Ailm*, or Pine, heralding the season of the evergreen trees when the deciduous trees drop their unpicked fruit and now-lifeless leaves. Though death is immanent, the tree is now funneling its vital energy deep into each fruit's core, to its seeds, so the cycle of life may be renewed beneath the protective blanket of fallen leaves. The decomposing husks of fruit both protects the seeds as they develop and feeds them as they breaks down, so that the old life nurtures the new life. Like lighting a fresh candle from the guttering flame of an old one, the spark of life is passed to the next generation to ensure the light itself never truly dies, only the current form carrying it.

In this Class of Seeding, the quest you have been journeying with shows you how it feeds the new quest that will emerge and reveal itself to you in your next flametending journey. It is the present quest itself that will reveal the new one at its core, and when it does, you will see and understand the next cycle your growth must take, and that vantage point will show you how far this journey has brought you and how it has transformed you. Now is the time to release the old story you were living through and the old identity that you wore as a part of it, just as the Oak of Mugna sheds its fruit and leaves at the end of its growth cycle.

As the old quest transforms to the new one while the dead and disintegrating fruit lies on the cold ground beneath a blanket of leaves, the land that is the tomb for the dying cycle transforms in a moment into the womb incubating renewed life, which will present a new story with new understandings and new opportunities for inner growth and illumination. This ogham class culminates the transformative flametending journey and creates space to incubate the next one to come.

The lines of characters of this ogham class are drawn horizontally, straight across the vertical stem from left to right, like branches of a winter tree bereft of leaves and relieved of its burden of ripe fruit. This class represents the season of winter when the dream of new life sleeps beneath the land, awaiting the time of renewal to emerge and begin a new cycle of growth.

A: **Ailm** – Pine – Transformation through Discernment
O: **Onn** – Furze – Transformation through Detachment
U: **Úr** – Heather – Transformation through Disintegration
E: **Edad** – Aspen – Transformation through Dreaming
I: **Idad** – Yew – Transformation through Regeneration

In the Scottish tradition recorded in the Carmina Gadelica, a rite performed on February 1st at St. Brìde's Day is welcoming a serpent rising from a knoll, like a precursor to the American Groundhog Day observed on February 2nd. Like the groundhog, the serpent awakens and arises from a winter hibernation when it senses a seasonal change in the land. Through this custom, I equate this serpent that sleeps through the winter with Brighid, whom I call in this season, the Dreamer, for, as the vital energies of the land hibernate and sleep through winter to then rise reborn at the arrival of spring, so does Brighid the Dreamer sleep beneath the earth, dreaming the dream of rebirth, then brings the dream to life with spring's awakening.

Here in this class of winter and seeding, the integration of the cycle's gleaned wisdom takes place. Just as we integrate experiences from our waking lives by dreaming as we sleep, in this class's work, we allow the deepest part of ourselves to embrace and store the illumination we discovered on our journey so we might call upon it in future moments of similar struggle or inquiry, and Brighid the Dreamer supports us in this work. Though we will soon move on to a new spiritual focus and its attending work, nothing gained will be lost, and in fact, it will directly feed the new inquiry which will manifest, just as the decomposing fruit which protected the seed becomes nourishment for the new seedling as it breaks free of its casing and stretches a root down like an umbilical cord to secure itself into the earth. This final class therefore witnesses life's great transformation of consciously releasing what is passing away and dreaming the new in order to step into the unknown in that brief but vitally pivotal heartbeat moment when the tomb of the earth housing the dying fruit cosmically transforms into the womb of the land incubating new life.

Brighid the Dreamer guides us in seeing the vision of the new quest held inside the one passing away so that we can discern what is gestating and preparing to rise to the surface of our conscious minds and careful attention. In this way, we release what no longer needs to hold our energy so it can be freed to support our next flametending journey. She guides us in allowing the current quest and its journey to die its natural death so we can give all our energy to the emerging journey and its latent illumination now awaiting us.

As you begin this final leg of your flametending journey, place your index and middle fingers on the outer corners of your eyes and recite this prayer to Brighid the Dreamer to guide your way:

Brighid the Dreamer, I call on you to walk with me through this ogham class to help me release what I no longer need so I can make space for what needs to become. Teach me to let go, be empty, and open my inner vision so I may discern the new spark that wants to awaken and take root within me. As it was, as it is, as it evermore shall be.

Vigil 16: Ailm – Pine

Keyword: Discernment

Word-ogham: *tosac frecrai* – beginning of an answer (MO)

All of our experiences offer illumination and wisdom, and once that light is shone on them for us to see, understand, and integrate, then we no longer require the experiences themselves, as we have learned what was required from them. They may now pass from our daily focus. You are now coming into the end of this flametending journey. The particular quest you worked with along the way carried a story around it, the story of how the quest brought you dis-ease. Now that you have transformed that dis-ease into power and joy, you need no longer walk in the story of dis-ease. It is no longer your story. In your newfound power and joy, you are making a new one.

Similarly, the mythic Oak of Mugna has served its spiritual purpose: to produce the fruits of wisdom to feed and guide those who come seeking it. So now, in its season of winter, its spent fruit withers on the branch. Likewise, your old story withers to make room for a new one. Releasing your old story releases the energy contained within it so it may feed the new story gestating within you, the way the dream of springtime gestates within the winter dream of Brighid the Dreamer. Now is the time to discern what that new story is so you can step out of the one passing away.

In your meditation, focus on the expired fruits of wisdom still hanging on the Oak of Mugna, and as you perceive them shriveling and dying, feel the old story you lived in similarly waning from the world. Feel deeply into the feeling of your new power and joy, then ask Brighid the Dreamer to help you discern what they want to become for you. Sit in this energy and open yourself to however it may want to speak to you, whether through visions, words, sounds, tunes, smells, ideas, sensations, etc. Stay with it until you are able to discern your new story that carries the seeds of the wisdom you gained through working with the old one. When you have clearly discerned it, thank Brighid for what you have received and record it in your flametending journal.

Journal Prompt: *What is the old story I am releasing and what is my new story gestating within me?*

Vigil 17: Ónn – Furze

Keyword: Detachment
Word-ogham: *congnaid ech* – helper of horses, i.e. the wheels of a chariot (MM)

Now that the fruit of wisdom has withered on the branch of the Oak of Mugna, the stem weakens and releases its hold. Just as the chariot moves on its wheels, the dying fruit with its new seeds of life inside suddenly moves into its next stage in its life cycle by detaching from the branch and falling to the ground.

This detachment of the fruit from the tree it has known signals the end of the life of the fruit. When the fruit withered on its branch in your previous meditation, so too did the story around your quest that was staying alive until you faced and integrated its lessons. Now that you have, the fruit can fall.

As the fruit falls, so can the last piece tying you to the outer husk of your quest: the identity of yourself you carried inside the story that was wrapped around your quest. The fruit no longer needs to be fruit, so it detaches from the tree that gave it form. Similarly, you can now detach from and release the identity you wore when you began your work with this quest and were wrapped inside its story. You have gleaned its meaning and become illuminated by its wisdom, and these processes have transformed you. You are no longer the same person you were when you began. It's important to remember that you are not the stories you have lived through, but the wisdom they gave you, and the soul that has grown in that wisdom.

In your meditation, envision the withered fruit of your story barely hanging from the Tree of Knowledge, and as you do, consider the way you identified inside the story you lived through and have been journeying through. Realize that your journey has matured your spirit and that you no longer need to remain attached to who you were. See in your mind's eye a symbol of this old and outworn identity that was part of the passing story and superimpose it onto the dying fruit. Now feel a breeze blowing up around you and watch as the fruit on the branch sways in the wind, then suddenly and easily detaches from the branch and falls to the earth below. As it falls, feel the identity that was you detaching from your energy and falling away. Sit with this moment to fully take in its sense of release and how it lightens your spirit. You need no longer carry it; you are now free to understand yourself as you truly are – a spark of the divine creative fire of the cosmos. Record your old identity's symbol in your flametending journal and how your spirit feels now that you have detached yourself from it.

Journal Prompt: *What identity am I detaching from that I wore inside my old story?*

Vigil 18: Úr – Heather

Keyword: Disintegration
Word-oghams:
forbbaíd ambí – shroud of the lifeless, i.e. soil (CC)
sílad cland – propagation and growing of plants, seeding up of plants (MO)

Two word-oghams are required for this character because two processes are taking place here simultaneously within a single act: as the life force travels from the mythic fruit of wisdom to the seed and detaches from the Oak of Mugna to fall to the earth, this final act of death simultaneously initiates new life by planting the seeds of the new tree within the land. The tomb of the earth that welcomes the dead becomes the womb of the land receiving new life.

But before this new life awakens, the last remnants of the dying form must disintegrate to fully break down its energies and make them available to feed the awaiting seed. This dissolution of form is also the final release of the form of your quest as you have shaped and journeyed through it, from formation, to examination, to illumination, as it is no longer needed. In the powerful and fertile soil of earth and soul, your quest and journey now disintegrate and rest in the quiet dark that is the void created by a dissolved form. This stage bookends the stage of formation, with which you began your journey. All forms eventually fall away, just as all journeys eventually conclude.

Though it is common to hear that we must release what is no longer needed to make room for the new, it can be unnerving to actually experience the void that this release creates. Humans have feared the void for its seemingly endless yawning of nothingness, afraid of being consumed by it and lost forever. But you have no need to fear it because unlike those still attached to their stories and identities, you have just consciously released yours. Now there is no fear of loss because nothing remains which can be lost.

Nature abhors a vacuum and works to quickly fill empty space to balance energy, but there is a moment when the void exists before it is filled. It is the pause between the exhale and the inhale, the pause between heartbeats. However, the void is not nothing, because it's impossible for nothing to exist. The universe isn't empty, it's full of energy, which can be neither created nor destroyed, so energy always exists. This is what the void contains: the cosmic energies from which all forms arise, which can be and is shaped into all the forms that have ever existed, presently exist, and will exist. The void is a place of mystery because the processes of disintegration and manifestation both occur here, in darkness and silence.

Releasing your outworn story and identity lightened your spirit, which in turn created space in it for new forms to fill. This moment right now is that space in your process of ongoing transformation when one journey has ended and the next one has yet to manifest. This is a time of pause and rest and feeling deeply into the experience of no experience, no activity, no movement, no work.

In your meditation, envision yourself like the fallen fruit, resting quietly in the earth at the end of its journey. Your quest has concluded and you no longer need to carry its weight. Its ending is like the death created by winter, a cosmic pause for rest before the rebirth of spring. Sit with Brighid the Dreamer, and breathe in the wordless mystery of the void. Bring this restive energy into your spirit sanctuary, your inner Cill Dara, and carry it with you after you finish your meditation.

Journal Prompt: *How does it feel to rest in void?*

Vigil 19: Edad – Aspen
Keyword: Visioning
Word-ogham: *bráthir beithi* – brother of birch (CC)

Brother of birch suggests another kind of beginning, as Birch begins the tree ogham. What is beginning now? The spark of life reborn in the void after the disintegration of the old form. Just as the dead fruit of the Oak of Mugna contains the seeds of new life within it, so your quest now passing away contains within it the seed of a new one. And as the fruit has fallen from the tree, the old message falls away to reveal the next one. And as the energy of the decaying fruit feeds the seeds it protected, the energy of the old quest feeds the seed of the new quest growing within it. The seed is what remains and with it, the cycle continues.

In your meditation, sit in this void and contemplate what

naturally follows from the quest that is receding; where does it suggest you go next? What direction does it reveal? The light of your inquiry and the torch of Brighid's dreaming will show you. And as the new quest appears in your inner vision, the future form its mythic seed will take is suggested. In that moment, in that space, breath, and heartbeat, the mythic realm of the tomb of the land housing the dead fruit of wisdom transforms into the terrestrial womb that gestates new life planted within it.

If you feel you need additional support to clearly see the vision of your new quest, revisit the Well of Wisdom and perform its meditation to help you discern it. When you have envisioned the new quest that you will journey with during your next flametending cycle, record it in your flametending journal.

Journal Prompt: *What is the new quest carried within the essence of the old one?*

Vigil 20: Idad – Yew
Keyword: Regeneration
Word-ogham: *sinem fedo* – oldest word/tree/letter, older than letters (MM)

Older than the tree ogham alphabet, even older than the trees themselves, is the cosmic cycle of life, death, and rebirth. All of our ancestors knew and expressed this knowledge in some sacred way within their cultures. Just as they witnessed the outer cycles that are solar, lunar, and terrestrial, they understood the inner cycles of spiritual growth and development and honored these as well. The flametending cycle can be engaged with as one such path of spiritual evolution, one cycle at a time, spiraling around and building upon the energy and wisdom of what came before, like continual reincarnations of the soul.

In this final beat of this cyclic dance, the planted seed and new quest swell with the energies fed to them by the dying forms that contained them, and as the seasonal cycle now turns toward the rising light and portal of new life, the swelling seeds of both the Oak of Mugna and your new quest crack open and send their first tentative roots down into the fertile soil of both land and soul. The dream within the seed begins its journey of manifestation, as does the quest it carries for you. In this moment, the energy of death is transformed into birth.

As you meditate, feel your new quest absorbing the remaining nourishing energy of the old one that has passed away, and contemplate how this nourishment feeds the form your new quest will take as it begins to root itself in your inner soul sanctuary, your Cill Dara, which will become enriched by the illumination found in this new spiritual journey you are about to embark on.

Journal Prompt: *How does the old quest feed the new one?*

You have completed a flametending cycle of twenty vigils with twenty ogham trees, through the four stages of development represented by the four classes of the ogham and the terrestrial seasons their opening trees suggest. You have walked each step with your quest and have come through transformed.

Take a moment to pause and appreciate the growth you have undergone and how it has affected you. As you transform, your soul inside you in its sanctuary glows brighter, and you yourself become a torch shining like a beacon for others, to inspire them toward their own spiritual journey and transformation. When we do the work, we all carry the Torch of Brighid.

Chapter 6

The Transformational Seasonal Journey
Your Year With Four Festivals & Five Trees

There is a fifth class of five extra ogham characters created some time after the feda, the primary twenty letters and four classes of the ogham alphabet, called the *forfeda*. Unlike the feda, their characters are not drawn as a collective and progressive set, but as unique characters each unto themselves, as they represent introduced sounds not originally found in the spoken Irish language. In this way, each one can stand alone in meaning, but they can also be viewed together as another symbolic cycle. Refer back to the image of the Ogham alphabet at the opening of the previous chapter to see these characters. Note that I do not use the letter P, as the sound was usually combined with the letter B and written as Beith, and the letter itself is infrequently used.

While the twenty characters of the feda are cycled through here as miniature inner journeys of spiritual growth, the forfeda can simultaneously be engaged with as the energies of greater development through the annual wheel of the Celtic seasons and their fire festivals. Further, the four seasons can be envisioned as the four arms of the Brighid's cross, which can be viewed as representing the four traditional Irish seasons of spring beginning with Imbolc (IMM-ulc) on February 1st, summer beginning with Bealtaine (BYELL-ten-uh) on May 1st, harvest/fall beginning with Lughnasadh (LOO-nuh-sah) on August 1st, and winter beginning with Samhain (SOW-in) on November 1st. Though the tradition of the Brighid's cross derives from native Irish Celtic Christianity, the symbol itself is an older, stylized sunwheel representing the sun turning us through the four seasons, so can make an apt symbol of and map for tracing our development through the seasonal cycle, should we choose to engage with it this way.

Brighid's Cross. Image by Lucya Starza, author of Candle Magic in the Pagan Portals series by Moon Books. Used with permission.

Just as we can shape and transform our spiritual lives through working with the flametending cycle, we can also shape and transform our temporal lives and greater development by moving consciously through the solar cycle. The encompassing solar cycle can also add another layer of influence to our work within the flametending cycles as the energies of the season add their color to the energies of our flametending work. The four faces of Brighid can guide us through this larger cycle when we undertake meditational journeys to connect with them at the beginnings of each season on the fire festival dates so Brighid can shine her torch of illumination and show us the way forward.

EA: **Ebad** – Elecampane – The Journey – Salmon of Knowledge & Sun of the Seasons
OI: **Óir** – Spindle Tree – Imbolc – Season of Formation
UI: **Uilleand** – Honeysuckle – Bealtaine – Season of Examination
IA: **Iphín** – Gooseberry – Lughnasadh – Season of Illumination
AE: **Emancholl** – Witch hazel – Samhain – Season of Transformation

The Journey: Ebad – Elecampane

Keyword: Journey
Word-ogham: *caínem éco*, fairest fish, most lovely of salmon (CC)

The salmon, this "fairest fish," is an apt symbol for the annual journey through the seasons. The salmon grows its body early in the year upon hatching from eggs, then moves out into the world as it undergoes its transformation from freshwater river creature to saltwater sea creature. Similarly, we begin each annual cycle with the freshness of new beginnings, making plans for new endeavors which then shape and change us as we enact and live through them. The salmon is also one of the penultimate symbols of wisdom in the Irish tradition: *Bradan Feasa*, the Salmon of Knowledge, that resides in the mythic Well of Wisdom, which in this representation can symbolize wisdom gained from both lived experience and reflection on those experiences.

We can align ourselves with the salmon's annual cycle of emergence and growth, journeying forth, returning home, and generating and incubating new life so we can draw the salmon's wisdom to us in every season of the year. The center of Brighid's cross can be envisioned as both the sun that turns the solar wheel and the well of wisdom wherein dwells the mythic Salmon of Knowledge from Irish tradition. This Well is always available to revisit along the journey whenever we feel the need to reconnect with inspiration and insight.

And Brighid too is part of this annual journey. Being a goddess of fire, this fire she represents can be equated with solar fire, and indeed, as noted throughout this book, an eleventh-century prayer to St Brigit refers to her as the *radiant fire of the sun*. When contemplating your solar journey, you can envision Brighid as the Sun herself, illuminating your way with her great torch in the sky.

Imbolc: Óir – Spindle Tree

Keyword: *Form, Gold*
Word-ogham: *lí crotha*, splendor of form (MO)
Season: Spring, Season of Formation
Face of Brighid: Brighid the Smith
Seasonal Contemplation: *How am I shaping the forms of myself and my unfolding path this year?*

Spring, which begins with the Gaelic feast of Imbolc on February 1st, is the season of growth and formation, when buried seeds awaken and the first signs of new life appear on the land. This is the time to put energy toward shaping the year and the life you want to live into the forms of your own choosing, and who you want to be as you live it. Brighid the Smith is the Shaper of Form. During the season of spring, you can connect with and channel her energy to become the Shaper of your goals, direction, and self. You can also connect with her throughout the season by asking her to bless your new endeavors and guide you as you proceed in shaping them.

While Óir is associated with the spindle tree, it also indicates ór, the Irish word for gold, a metal, which also connects this ogham character with Brighid the Smith, who uses raw materials to shape and fashion something beautiful and valuable with the transformative power of fire. By connecting with Brighid the

Smith at Imbolc, the beginning of spring, you can tap into and channel this power of shaping to begin consciously forming your emerging year.

Spring is also the season when salmon eggs that had incubated in a riverbed though winter now hatch and young salmon grow into their adult form in their still pools to prepare for their coming journey. Hatching and growing your yearly dreams, goals, and intentions aligns with this stage of the salmon's development. And as you move through your new experiences, they will similarly shape and mature you for the greater work to come.

Connect with the energies of springtime and Brighid the Smith at Imbolc with the following Imbolc Meditation.

Imbolc Meditation with Brighid the Smith
Find a comfortable and quiet place to sit or lie down for about an hour where you won't be disturbed. You can read through the meditation beforehand and follow it as you meditate or record it and play it back to guide you.

Begin by lighting your Brighid candle on your Brighid shrine with the Flame-kindling Prayer:

Brighid,
Excellent, Exalted One,
Bright, golden, quickening flame –
Shine your blessings on us from the Otherworld –
You,
Radiant fire of the Sun.[1]

Make an offering to Brighid of seasonally available milk and/or grain products. Now settle your body and ground yourself with three deep, cleansing breaths, close your eyes, and open your inner vision to the following meditation.

Envision yourself standing at the opening of the spiral hedge leading to your inner flame temple. It is dawn. You are wearing a cloak to keep yourself warm and carrying a lantern to light your way where darkness still lingers. Turning your back to the spiral hedge, you follow a path before you. It leads to a river with a footbridge over it in the near distance and when you reach the bridge, you step onto it and cross the river.

Once on the other side, you enter a forest. As you continue following the path, you begin to sense the energy of the land thrumming beneath your feet, so you draw it up into your Cauldron of Warming with your breath and feel its energy move within you. Your breathing falls into rhythm with your steps. Soon the path exits the forest and opens out onto a wide plain. As you traverse it, you continue feeding your Cauldron of Warming with the awakening fire deep within the land. Up ahead of you, you see your destination – a faery hill with a fully-crowned oak tree standing on its peak: it is the Oak of Mugna, the mythic Tree of Knowledge. You notice how its bare branches appear to be softly shimmering in the frosty air.

As you approach the hill, you see a spiral path cut into it leading to the top. Stepping onto it, you follow it around the sides of the hill and when you arrive at the top, you see that you are not alone; other celebrants have also come to welcome Spring and receive the blessing of Brighid. Near the great oak sits a small forge with a fire inside it and a basket of taper candles placed nearby. As you see the others have done, you select a candle and light it from the forge's fire, then carry it with you and join them where they stand together around the tree, gazing up at it as you all hold the power of the land in your inner cauldrons with a soft hum.

As the morning sun appears on the horizon and rises up into the sky, the sound of the hum grows louder, which then gives way to a chant calling out to Brighid to honor her on her special day:

Triumphant Brigid,
Glory of the season,
Noble sunrise,
Broad-spreading flame!
Awake from your sleep,
Return to the land,
O Victorious Brigid,
Living One of Life![2]

You feel Spring's first sunrays bathe your face in its warm glow. As you stand with everyone calling to Brighid, a ball of silvery light appears from its crown and slowly floats to the ground. When it touches the land, it transforms into Brighid, whom the people call the Faery Queen, bearing the Cup of Wisdom everyone has come to sip from.[3] In the hush that follows, Brighid speaks. As you listen to her words, you breathe their energy into your Cauldron of Motion and feel it awaken:

I am older than Brigit of the Mantle,
I put songs and music on the wind
Before ever the bells of the chapels
Were rung in the West
Or heard in the East.
I am Brighid-nam-Bratta:
Brigit of the Mantle,

I am also Brighid-Muirghin-na-tuinne:
Brigit, Conception of the Waves,

And Brighid-sluagh,
Brigit of the Faery Host,

Brighid-nan-sitheachseang,
Brigit of the Slim Faery Folk,

Brigid-Binne-Bheule-
Ihuchd-nan-trusganan-uaine,
Brigit the Melodious Mouthed
Of the Tribe of the Green Mantles.

And I am older than Aone, Friday
And as old as Luan, Monday

And in Tir-na-h'oige my name is
Suibhal: Mountain Traveler,

And in Tir-fo-thuinn, Country of the Waves,
It is Cu-gorm: Gray Hound,

And in Tir-na-h'oise,
Country of Ancient Years,
It is Sireadh-thall: Seek Beyond.

And I have been a breath in your heart,
And the day has its feet to it
That will see me coming
Into the hearts of men and women
Like a flame upon dry grass,
Like a flame of wind in a great wood.[4]

After she speaks, Brighid begins to circulate around the crowd with her Cup of Wisdom, offering everyone a sip. Everyone extinguishes their candles now that the Imbolc sun has risen and awakened the land. She slowly works her way closer until she is standing before you, proffering her Cup. Quietly, you ask her to reveal to you a symbol of the shape of your emerging soul-self in this new year. She smiles into your eyes and nods in acknowledgement of your request. You then take a deep drink from her Cup of Wisdom. As Brighid moves on to the next celebrant, you spread your cloak on the dew-damp grass and settle yourself on it to receive the vision from her elixir. The drink warms and overturns your Cauldron of Knowledge and slowly, as your body further relaxes, you see a symbol begin to take form, and understand it to be the essence of your emerging self in this renewed season of growth.

Some time passes until you feel you have received what was meant for you. Then, when you sit up and look around, you notice that the others there are also beginning to stir from their visions. As everyone's attention returns to Brighid, she calls out a blessing:

> *Grace upward over you,*
> *Grace downward over you.*
> *Grace of the love of the skies be yours,*
> *Grace of the love of the stars be yours,*
> *Grace of the love of the moon be yours,*
> *Grace of the love of the sun be yours.*[5]

You call out thanks to her with the others and watch as she transforms back into a silvery bubble and floats back up into the crown of the great oak tree.

With joy and a lightness of spirit, you walk the spiral path back down the hill and notice how it is now blanketed with low, nodding heads of tiny white snowdrop flowers. Then you cross the sunny plain and see how it is now dotted with grazing, fluffy-white ewes and new lambs, and pass through the forest that is now ringing with birdsong to then reach the footbridge and cross the river to the other side and arrive where you began, at the opening of the spiral hedge that leads to your fire temple.

Take three deep breaths now, and with each one, see the scene before you fade away and become aware of your body. Then slowly open your eyes and stretch to fully return to yourself in your room before your Brighid shrine.

Journal everything you experienced in your meditation, including the symbol Brighid showed you when you drank from her Cup of Wisdom. Afterward, extinguish your Brighid candle and set your offerings outdoors.

Now that you have the symbol, find or fashion an image of it to place on your shrine to inspire your work in the coming months. Spend the spring season embodying the form of your newly-emerged soul-self.

Bealtaine: Uillean – Honeysuckle

Keyword: *sweetness of life*
Word-ogham: *túthmar fid*, fragrant tree (MM)
Season: Summer, Season of Examination
Face of Brighid: Brighid the Healer
Seasonal Contemplation: *How can I best pursue and practice balance so I can best bring my gifts to the world?*

After the Smith's shaping, Brighid the Healer examines the new form to ensure it achieves and maintains inner and outer equilibrium, a balanced state of health, so the True Self can blossom, then breathe life into the created form to fulfill its purpose in the world. Connect with Brighid the Healer so you can embody this energy to help you assess where balance is needed and how to create it to best further your endeavors. Disease is disequilibrium and the Healer knows how to correct imbalances to achieve optimal health. The True Self can only blossom when the whole being is balanced.

Summer is the season when the created form of ourselves and our year's goals and dreams are fully in motion to attract desirable experiences while we present our gifts to the world. Summer begins in the Gaelic calendar with the feast of Bealtaine on May 1st, traditionally when the hawthorn blooms, whose flowers are medicine for the heart. Summer is also the season when the grown salmon leave their nesting ground, migrate downriver, and enter their great journey in the sea. Your year's journey is similarly underway as you work with the energies you have put into motion to create your annual adventure. These are the experiences that will provide you with important knowledge and wisdom so long as you maintain your awareness as you live them.

You can connect with Brighid the Healer at Bealtaine with the following meditation.

Bealtaine Meditation with Brighid the Healer

Find a comfortable and quiet place to sit or lie down for about an hour where you won't be disturbed. You can read through the meditation beforehand and follow it as you meditate or record it and play it back to guide you.

Begin by lighting your Brighid candle on your Brighid shrine with the Flame-kindling Prayer:

Brighid,
Excellent, Exalted One,
Bright, golden, quickening flame –
Shine your blessings on us from the Otherworld –
You,
Radiant fire of the Sun.

Make an offering to Brighid of seasonally available milk and/or grain products. Now settle your body and ground yourself with three deep breaths, then close your eyes and open your inner vision to the following scene.

You are standing at the opening of the spiral hedge that leads to your inner flame temple. It is a dark night. You are wearing a cloak to keep yourself warm and carrying a lantern to light your way. Turning your back to the hedge, you step onto a path before you that leads to a river in the near distance. You follow the path toward it, and when you reach it, you see a footbridge leading over it which you step onto and cross the river.

Once on the other side, you enter a forest. As you continue following the path, you begin to sense the land's energy thrumming beneath your feet. With your breath, you draw it up into your Cauldron of Warming as you walk and feel it awakening this energy center. As it does, you are reminded of the bonfire to be built at your destination, so you begin collecting fallen branches along the path for firewood.

Soon the path exits the forest and opens onto a wide plain beneath a sky lit by a full moon. As you walk, you continue breathing the power of the land into your Cauldron of Warming. Up ahead of you, you see your destination – a faery hill where an immense oak tree stands on its peak. The tree appears to be softly glowing in the night. As you approach the hill, you see a spiral path cut into its sides leading to the top and follow it.

When you arrive at the top of the hill, you see that you are not alone; other celebrants have also come to welcome Summer and receive the blessing of Brighid. A bonfire is being prepared. Like the others are doing, you place your kindling on the growing stack of wood, then join them in standing in a ring around the wood. You all hum softly together to hold and build the rising energies of the land together in your Cauldrons of Warming, channeling it up through your bodies to call up the first sunrise of summer. Behind the circle, a smaller fire quietly burns in the night.

In time, the chill in the air deepens and streaks of faint yellow and pink begin to light the eastern horizon. Excitedly, you each pick up a stick from the bonfire stack and light it from the small fire. Then, standing around the massive pile of wood, you all call out together to the Sun:

Hail to you, O Sun of the Seasons,
As you traverse the lofty skies!

Your way is strong on the wing of the heavens,
You are the glowing Mother of the Stars!
You have your lying down in the destroying ocean,
Without harming, without fear.
You rise on the serene hillcrest,
Like a Queenly Woman in bloom![6]

As you all chant this prayer to the sun, you see the sky begin to brighten. Soon the sun's disk appears on the lip of the horizon, then slowly rises over and floats above it. At that moment, you and the others toss your lit torches onto the bonfire stack and watch it burst into flames that seem to reach the heavens! Summer has come! As the sun rises up into the sky, with several breaths, you breathe its warm energy down into you Cauldron of Knowledge and feel it awaken this energy center behind your inner eye.

You feel the twin fires of the land and sun merge within you as you stand between them, on the hill and beneath the sky. As the rays of the sun touch the flames of the bonfire, you now turn with everyone toward the great oak tree and slowly approach it. It is in full leaf and bearing three kinds of flowers. A ball of silvery light appears from its crown and slowly floats to the ground. When it touches the land, it transforms into Brighid, whom the people call the Faery Queen, bearing her Cup of Wisdom. You feel your heart open to her and your Cauldron of Motion turn upward inside you to receive her energy. A hush falls over the crowd and Brighid speaks:

I am older than Brigit of the Mantle,
I put songs and music on the wind
Before ever the bells of the chapels
Were rung in the West
Or heard in the East.
I am Brighid-nam-Bratta:
Brigit of the Mantle,

I am also Brighid-Muirghin-na-tuinne:
Brigit, Conception of the Waves,

And Brighid-sluagh,
Brigit of the Faery Host,

Brighid-nan-sitheachseang,
Brigit of the Slim Faery Folk,

Brigid-Binne-Bheule-
Ihuchd-nan-trusganan-uaine,
Brigit the Melodious Mouthed
Of the Tribe of the Green Mantles.

And I am older than Aone (Friday)
And as old as Luan (Monday)

And in Tir-na-h'oige my name is
Suibhal: Mountain Traveler,

And in Tir-fo-thuinn, Country of the Waves,
It is Cu-gorm: Gray Hound,

And in Tir-na-h'oise,
Country of Ancient Years,
It is Sireadh-thall: Seek Beyond.

And I have been a breath in your heart,
And the day has its feet to it
That will see me coming
Into the hearts of men and women
Like a flame upon dry grass,
Like a flame of wind in a great wood.

Brighid holds her Cup of Wisdom up to the rising sun to capture the energy of its rays, then begins to circulate around the crowd, offering everyone a sip. Slowly she works her way closer until she is standing before you, proffering her Cup. Quietly, you ask her to reveal to you a symbol of what would best bring you balance, equilibrium, and vitality through the summer season to help you bloom and bring your gifts to the world as you actualize your dreams. You ask her to share with you how you can embody her ability as The Healer so you can bring this healing balance to your life. She smiles into your eyes and nods in acknowledgment of your request, then you take a deep drink from her Cup of Wisdom. As she moves on to the next celebrant, you reach down to the grass at your feet and wet your fingers with the dew there and anoint your closed eyelids with it to strengthen your inner sight, then spread out your cloak and lie down on it to receive the elixir's vision. As the power of the drink upturns and fully opens your Cauldron of Knowledge, you see a symbol take shape and how you must use it to balance yourself and maintain your equilibrium.

After a while, when you feel you have received what is meant for you, you look up and around and notice that the others are also beginning to stir from their visions. As everyone's attention returns to Brighid, she calls out a blessing:

> *Grace upward over you,*
> *Grace downward over you.*
> *Grace of the love of the skies be yours,*
> *Grace of the love of the stars be yours,*
> *Grace of the love of the moon be yours,*
> *Grace of the love of the sun be yours.*

You all call out thanks to her and watch as she transforms back into a silvery bubble and floats back up into the crown of the great oak tree. With peace and gratitude in your heart, you walk the spiral path back down the hill and walk across the plain bathed in bright sunlight beneath a blue sky. Further along, you see hawthorn trees blooming at the edge of the wood you walked through on your way to the faery hill. You follow the path into the forest and enjoy the sound of birdsong falling from the treetops. As the path emerges from the trees, you walk over the footbridge to cross the river and arrive where you began, at the opening of the spiral hedge leading to your fire temple.

Take three deep breaths and as you do, see the scene before you slowly fade and become aware of your body. Then slowly open your eyes and stretch to come fully back to yourself in your room before your Brighid shrine.

Journal everything you experienced in your meditation, including the symbol that Brighid showed you when you drank from her Cup of Wisdom. Afterward, extinguish your Brighid candle and set your offerings outdoors.

Now that you have the symbol, find or fashion an image of it to place on your shrine to inspire your work over the coming months. Spend your summer season embodying Brighid the Healer by paying close attention to what unbalances and rebalances your soul, preserves your mental equilibrium, and spiritually vitalizes you so that you can maintain an optimum state of inner health to actualize your dreams and bring your gifts to the world.

Lughnasadh: Iphín – Gooseberry

Keyword: *Bounty*
Word-ogham: *amram mlais* – most wonderful taste (MO)
Season: Harvest, Season of Illumination
Face of Brighid: Brighid the Poet
Seasonal Contemplation: *What bounty of learning do I take from my work, and what deeper understandings are illuminated from my process of becoming this year?*

The harvest season is when we reap the bounty of what we have sown and tended throughout the seasons of growth, and of what has naturally matured of its own accord. The bounty gained from your lived experiences is knowledge, which, when reflected on, offers wisdom. Wisdom illuminates the insights this learning provides, which in turn further informs our choices and actions so our work this year can fully ripen into its intended purpose.

This also sees the season when the salmon return from the sea to their spawning grounds to offer up their bounty of new life for another generation, the harvest of their great journey with all its experiences. Similarly, we too now see some tangible results of our experiences and pause to consider what insights they reveal.

After the season of outward growth and expansion, we now turn back into ourselves to draw the energy of our experiences inward to nourish us. Brighid the Poet shows us both the knowledge we are harvesting and what its deeper meaning is and how it furthers our understanding and development. Illumination also reveals the path forward from here, how to work with these insights we reap as we begin to spiral into the introspective half of the year.

You can connect with Brighid the Poet at the Gaelic feast of Lughnasadh through the following meditation.

Lughnasadh Meditation with Brighid the Poet
Find a comfortable and quiet place to sit or lie down for about an hour where you won't be disturbed. You can read through the meditation beforehand and follow it as you meditate or record it and play it back to guide you.

Begin by lighting your Brighid candle on your Brighid shrine with the Flame-kindling Prayer:

Brighid,
Excellent, Exalted One,
Bright, golden, quickening flame –

Shine your blessings on us from the Otherworld –
You,
Radiant fire of the Sun.

Make an offering to Brighid of seasonally available milk and/or grain products. Now settle your body and ground yourself with three deep breaths, then close your eyes and open your inner sight to the following vision.

Envision yourself standing at the opening of the spiral hedge leading to your inner flame temple. It is a bright, pleasantly warm day and you are carrying a small bouquet of wildflowers. You turn your back to the hedge and begin treading a path before you leading to a river in the near distance with a footbridge over it. You walk toward it, and when you reach the bridge, you step onto it and cross the river.

Once on the other side, you enter a forest. As you continue following the path, you begin to sense the land's energy thrumming beneath your feet and draw it up into your Cauldron of Warming with your breath. You feel your inhaling and exhaling falling into rhythm with your steps.

Soon the path exits the forest and opens onto a wide plain of tall grains growing beneath a deep blue sky. As you walk, you continue breathing the fiery energy in the core of the land into your Cauldron of Warming. Up ahead of you, you see your destination – a faery hill with a fully-fruited oak tree standing on its peak, producing apples, acorns, and hazelnuts all at once. As you approach the hill, you see a spiral path cut into its sloping sides leading to the top. You follow it. When you reach the top, you see that you are not alone; other celebrants have also come to welcome the Harvest and receive the blessing of Brighid. They are gathered around a dug pit which is lined with wildflowers brought by others, laid inside as an offering to Brighid and a signal that summer's growth is coming to a close. You place your bouquet inside with the others and then stand together with the crowd around the great oak tree, holding the fire of the land together in your Cauldrons of Warming with a soft hum.

Suddenly the sound of bells is heard, and you all look up to see a ball of silvery light appearing from the tree's crown, then slowly floating to the ground. When it touches the land, it transforms into Brighid, whom the people call the Faery Queen, bearing her Cup of Wisdom. At the sight of her, you feel a rush of warm emotion in your heart center, your Cauldron of Motion, and it opens to receive her energy as she speaks:

I am older than Brigit of the Mantle,
I put songs and music on the wind
Before ever the bells of the chapels
Were rung in the West
Or heard in the East.
I am Brighid-nam-Bratta:
Brigit of the Mantle,

I am also Brighid-Muirghin-na-tuinne:
Brigit, Conception of the Waves,

And Brighid-sluagh,
Brigit of the Faery Host,

Brighid-nan-sitheachseang,
Brigit of the Slim Faery Folk,

Brigid-Binne-Bheule-
Ihuchd-nan-trusganan-uaine,
Brigit the Melodious Mouthed
Of the Tribe of the Green Mantles.

And I am older than Aone (Friday)
And as old as Luan (Monday)

And in Tir-na-h'oige my name is
Suibhal: Mountain Traveler,

And in Tir-fo-thuinn, Country of the Waves,
It is Cu-gorm: Gray Hound,

And in Tir-na-h'oise,
Country of Ancient Years,
It is Sireadh-thall: Seek Beyond.

And I have been a breath in your heart,
And the day has its feet to it
That will see me coming
Into the hearts of men and women
Like a flame upon dry grass,
Like a flame of wind in a great wood.

Quietly, you contemplate what your process of shaping and healing and blossoming and creating has taught you so far, what you have learned up to this point. Slowly Brighid begins moving among the crowd, offering her Cup of Wisdom. When she approaches, you see that the liquid inside her cup is a deep red color and hazelnuts are floating on its surface. You ask Brighid to impart a symbol to you showing you the deeper meaning in the wisdom you are harvesting now, and how this can further guide you and nourish your growth. As you sip from the cup, you feel your Cauldron of Knowledge turn upright to receive her visions. You lie down in the warm grass and open yourself to receive Brighid's illumination as she guides you in how to embody the Poet to discern insight from your experiences thus far.

After a time, when you feel you have received what Brighid wants you to know, you look up and around to see that the other celebrants are also coming out of their visions. As everyone's attention returns to Brighid, she calls out a blessing:

Grace upward over you,
Grace downward over you.
Grace of the love of the skies be yours,
Grace of the love of the stars be yours,
Grace of the love of the moon be yours,
Grace of the love of the sun be yours.

You call out thanks to her with the others and watch as she transforms back into a silvery bubble and floats back up into the crown of the great oak tree. With understanding and gratitude in your heart, you spiral your way back down the hill, then walk across the plain, now golden as the grains have ripened for harvesting. You follow the path into the forest and enjoy the windsong playing in the leafy canopy above. As the path emerges from the trees, you walk over the footbridge to cross the river, then arrive where you began, at the opening of the spiral hedge leading to your fire temple. Stand there for a moment and take in three deep breaths, seeing the scene before you fade with each one, while becoming more aware of your body and the sensation of the surface beneath it. Then slowly open your eyes and stretch to bring yourself fully back to your body in your room before your Brighid shrine.

Journal everything you experienced in your meditation, everything Brighid imparted to you when you drank from her Cup of Wisdom seeking illumination. Afterward, extinguish your Brighid candle and set your offerings outdoors.

Now that you have the symbol, find or fashion an image of it to place on your shrine to inspire your work over the coming months. Spend your Harvest season embodying Brighid the Poet by engaging with the bounty of insight you've been given in whatever ways you are guided to. In this way, you will be tasting of the Fruits of Wisdom throughout the season.

Samhain: Emancholl – Witch Hazel

Keyword: *Dreaming*
Word-ogham: *lúad sáethaig*, expression of a weary one (MM)
Season: Winter, Season of Transformation
Face of Brighid: Brighid the Dreamer
Seasonal Contemplation: *What lessons am I now ready to release and what is the essence of the new dream wanting to take shape for the coming year?*

The salmon have returned to their hatching pools and have lain their eggs, which are now incubating and hibernating through the cold darkness of winter that is like a cosmic womb. During this season, as did the tired salmon at the end of their annual journey, we can both release what we no longer need to carry, and plant new dreams within us to gestate until spring.

Similarly, Brighid becomes the Dreamer at Samhain and retires like the land's life force to tend the smoored fire of the earth's energy as it burns low through the long night of winter. There, she sleeps and dreams of the new life that will emerge in Spring at Imbolc. You can embody Brighid the Dreamer by contemplating your passing year's experiences so they can transform into new dreams. In this space of time between seasonal death and rebirth, the insights gleaned from your endeavors will transform you with newfound wisdom, which will then become the light that guides you when you put your new dreams into motion at the awakening of spring.

You can connect with Brighid the Dreamer at Samhain through the following meditation.

Samhain Meditation with Brighid the Dreamer
Find a comfortable and quiet place to sit or lie down for about an hour where you won't be disturbed. You can read through the meditation beforehand and follow it as you meditate or record it

and play it back to guide you.

Begin by lighting your Brighid candle on your Brighid shrine with the Flame-kindling Prayer:

Brighid,
Excellent, Exalted One,
Bright, golden, quickening flame –
Shine your blessings on us from the Otherworld –
You,
Radiant fire of the Sun.

Make an offering to Brighid of seasonally available milk and/or grain products. Now settle your body and ground yourself with three deep breaths, then close your eyes and open your inner sight to the following vision.

Envision yourself standing at the opening of the spiral hedge that leads to your inner fire temple. It is deep night. You are wearing a cloak to warm you and carrying a lantern to light your way. You turn your back to the hedge and begin treading a path before you leading to a nearby river in the distance with a footbridge over it. You walk toward it, and when you reach the bridge, you step onto it and cross the river.

Once on the other side, you enter a forest. As you continue following the path, you begin to sense the land's energy thrumming beneath your feet and breathe it up into your Cauldron of Warming. You notice how your inhaling and exhaling falling into rhythm with your steps.

Soon the path exits the forest and opens onto a wide plain of dried stalks of harvested grains barely visible in the lights of your lantern and the sliver of a waning crescent moon above. As you walk, you continue breathing the fiery energy inside the land into your Cauldron of Warming. Up ahead of you, you see your destination – a faery hill with a great oak tree standing on its peak, bare branches reaching to the sky. As you approach the hill, you see a path that winds around behind it. You follow it to the back of the hill where you find a doorway opening into the side of the hill. You step inside.

The space inside is a tall, round cave and a fire is lit in its center. Around it are arrayed pallets and blankets on which other celebrants are seated. You find an empty one and seat yourself there among them. After you settle yourself, you meditate on the central fire and draw its energy into your Cauldron of Motion with your breath. You take several breaths until you feel that your inner cauldron and this fire are connected and burning together.

A low humming arises from the crowd around you. You join in. As the sound grows, a ball of silvery light rises up from the fire and slowly floats to the ground. When it touches down, it transforms into Brighid, whom the people call the Faery Queen, bearing her Cup of Wisdom. A hush falls over the crowd, then Brighid speaks:

I am older than Brigit of the Mantle,
I put songs and music on the wind
Before ever the bells of the chapels
Were rung in the West
Or heard in the East.
I am Brighid-nam-Bratta:
Brigit of the Mantle,

I am also Brighid-Muirghin-na-tuinne:
Brigit, Conception of the Waves,

And Brighid-sluagh,
Brigit of the Faery Host,

Brighid-nan-sitheachseang,
Brigit of the Slim Faery Folk,

Brigid-Binne-Bheule-
Ihuchd-nan-trusganan-uaine,
Brigit the Melodious Mouthed
Of the Tribe of the Green Mantles.

And I am older than Aone (Friday)
And as old as Luan (Monday)

And in Tir-na-h'oige my name is
Suibhal: Mountain Traveler,

And in Tir-fo-thuinn, Country of the Waves,
It is Cu-gorm: Gray Hound,

And in Tir-na-h'oise,
Country of Ancient Years,
It is Sireadh-thall: Seek Beyond.

And I have been a breath in your heart,
And the day has its feet to it
That will see me coming
Into the hearts of men and women
Like a flame upon dry grass,
Like a flame of wind in a great wood.

Quietly, you contemplate the lessons you have gained wisdom from this year that you no longer need to carry with you, and begin to wonder what the new year will hold when the cycle turns to growth once again. Slowly Brighid begins moving around the crowd, offering her Cup of Wisdom. When she approaches you, you ask Brighid to help you release with gratitude the lessons you have outgrown and their residual energies and experiences so the space necessary for new dream to grow within can be made. For like the fallen and decaying fruit from the tree, its decomposing energy will nourish the seeds within of new life over the months to come. Then you ask her for a symbol of how the wisdom you have harvested will feed the dream of the new year as it gestates within you through winter. She gazes deeply into your eyes and nods to acknowledge your request.

As you sip from her cup, you feel the energy from its elixir overturn your Cauldron of Knowledge so it may be filled with visions from Brighid. You then lie back on your pallet of blankets to see what Brighid has to show you.

After a time, when you feel you have received what Brighid wants you to know, you look up and around to see that the other celebrants are also coming out of their visions. As everyone's attention returns to Brighid, she calls out a blessing:

Grace upward over you,
Grace downward over you.
Grace of the love of the skies be yours,
Grace of the love of the stars be yours,
Grace of the love of the moon be yours,
Grace of the love of the sun be yours.

You call out thanks to her with the others and watch as she transforms back into a silvery bubble and floats back into the fire in the center of the cave. With the lightness of release and a spirit full of dreams, you make your way out of the faery hill, across the stark plain, and through the forest littered with fallen leaves until you reach the river and walk over the footbridge to arrive where you began, at the opening of the spiral hedge leading to your fire temple. Stand there for a moment and take in three deep breaths to let the scene before you fade and the sensations of your body and the surface beneath it come into your awareness. Then slowly open your eyes and stretch to bring yourself fully back to your body in your room before your Brighid shrine.

Journal everything you experienced in your meditation, everything Brighid imparted to you when you drank from her Cup of Wisdom. Afterward, extinguish your Brighid candle and set your offerings outdoors.

Now that you have the symbol, find or fashion an image of it to place on your shrine to inspire your work over the coming months. Spend your Winter season embodying Brighid the Dreamer by releasing energies no longer needed and channeling them and the wisdom you gained from the year's experiences into dreaming new visions to incubate until Spring returns to shape into new dreams of formation, examination, and illumination.

Endnotes:

1. Reworking of an eleventh-century prayer to St. Brigit. Previously published by the author in *Brigid: Sun of Womanhood*, edited by Patricia Monaghan.
2. Inspired by a prayer to St. Brigit called, "Brigit Búadach/ Victorious Brigit," from the *Miscellanea Hibernica*, translated by Kuno Meyers.
3. Inspired by the tale of "The Maiden Queen of Wisdom" in the endnotes of the *Carmina Gadelica, Songs of the Gaels*, collected and translated by Alexander Carmichael.
4. "Brigit Speaks," by Fiona MacLeod.
5. "Blessing," from the *Carmina Gadelica*.
6. "Sun Prayer," from the *Carmina Gadelica*.

Chapter 7

The Transformational Imbolc Advent
Awakening from the Long Dark

The word *advent* means, arriving, appearing, or coming. An advent is a time of inner preparation for a grand arrival, or, in cyclic time, an anticipated return. In the traditional Gaelic seasonal calendar, Imbolc is the festival at the beginning of February that celebrates the beginning of springtime. In the Irish Catholic calendar, the day is known as St. Brigit's Day, and so Brighid has become inexorably connected with Imbolc and spring's return of the season of growth. Special crosses are woven from rushes and hung in homes to ensure her blessings on their inhabitants for the coming year.

In Scottish tradition, the Catholic celebration is called Brìde's Day. St. Brìde is welcomed into prepared homes so she may bring prosperity for the year to all who dwell within. The Brìde's Day traditions recorded by folklorist Alexander Carmichael in *The Carmina Gadelica*, or Songs of the Gaels, include prayers said to a serpent that was said to rise from a hill on this day, correlating with the beginning of this Gaelic season of spring:

The serpent shall come from the hole,
I will not molest the serpent,
Nor will the serpent molest me.

The serpent would have been hibernating underground through winter and would also be very sensitive to the shifts in energy moving with awakening and regrowing roots and changes in temperature commensurate with lengthening daylight. Sometimes the serpent is personified and addressed as royalty:

The noble queen will come from the knoll,
I will not molest the noble queen,
Nor will the noble queen molest me.

Just as some equate St. Bride with the goddess Brighid, we might view this serpent as an expression of Brighid as the vital energy of the land slumbering underground through winter to awaken and arise at springtime. The spirit of the saint herself was said in Scotland to walk the land the night before her feast day, bringing blessings to the homes that prepared for her by creating ikons of her set near their hearths and calling out to her from their doorways that her bed had been prepared for her.

As flametenders for Brighid, we can anticipate Brighid's annual return at Imbolc on February 1st by practicing an advent tradition, similar to the Christian tradition of observing an advent season in anticipation of the birth of Christ at Christmas. During this time of advent, we can prepare our souls and our hearths to welcome her when she arrives at Imbolc to renew them both, just as springtime, the season of regeneration, renews the land's growth. In this sense, we can commune with Brighid in the weeks leading up to Imbolc to guide us in both releasing what we no longer need to carry into the new season and considering what we might spiritually bring into the world as the land and sun rebirth their energies below and above us. In this way, Brighid's transformational fire can work within us, alchemizing the dreams of winter into the new creations of the coming year, and renewing our energy and inspiration for that work ahead.

Just as the sun slowly rises over the mound, so too can Brighid's fires slowly rise within us, warming and preparing us for her grand return, like the sun gradually bursting into full bloom. The Imbolc Advent takes place over the four Sundays preceding Imbolc, February 1st, and culminates in a celebratory ritual and meditation on Imbolc morning. Through these advent experiences, you will keep pace with Brighid's advancing return, then burst into bloom yourself as her presence finally, fully extends over the land.

Please note that this Imbolc Advent is not derived from any traditional Celtic practice, but does draw on traditional Brighidine lore, explored in a fresh way, to point us toward our soul's eternal flame within and how Brighid can help us tend it.

Preparation

Set aside time during the four Sundays prior to Imbolc, and the evening before and morning of. Each Sunday will resemble the steadily growing glow of a rising sun, which will finally summit into glory on Imbolc morn. You will need 30 to 60 minutes for each advent meditation, depending on how much time you need to delve into it, or how deeply you go.

Place five candle holders in any formation you like on either your Brighid shrine or in another set-aside space. Arranging them in the form of a Brighid's cross, with four candles set out as arms and the fifth in the center, is especially apt if you have room to do so. For each advent meditation, you will need candles in each holder, a means to light them, an offering bowl, and an offering (grain products or fermented beverages, and a dairy product on Imbolc morn), and your flametending journal for recording your responses to each week's questions for contemplation and your visions from the weekly meditations. Have everything ready and within reach before you begin.

First Sunday – Brighid the Dreamer

At the beginning of the Imbolc Advent, Brighid as the land's life force lies slumbering in the darkest depth of winter, dreaming the dream of springtime. As she does, so do we. But now, we begin to stir with the first whispers of movement toward the light.

To begin your meditation, welcome Brighid by leaving her an offering on her shrine and lighting one of your five advent candles with the Flame-kindling Prayer:

Brighid,
Excellent, Exalted One,
Bright, golden, quickening flame –
Shine your blessings on us from the Otherworld –
You,
Radiant fire of the Sun.

Take three deep, slow breaths to center and ground yourself, then perform the Mantle of Brighid exercise to fully open yourself to her energies in preparation for the Advent work.

Advent Work: The Serpent in the Knoll

In the Gaelic tradition of Scotland, Brìde's Day, as St. Brigit's Day is known there, is said to be the time when the waxing energy of the land appears in the form of a serpent rising from a faery hill. Because the serpent lies close to the heartbeat of the land, it knows when the power of the land quickens, and hence when the time is right to emerge. Before it does, it lies in winter darkness, as you yourself presently sit in the heart of winter's dark.

The serpent initially renews itself by shedding its old skin so it will be prepared to return to the land in full power. In your journal, consider what you might shed so you too can soon step into the growing year in your full power.

What holds you back? What constricts your growth? What impedes your path?

Contemplate and answer these questions in your flametending journal. Then close your eyes, take three deep breaths to clear your mind, and open your inner sight to the following vision.

You are the serpent, slumbering and dreaming beneath and

inside the cold, wintry knoll. You feel the darkness of both underground and winter surrounding you. Then you begin to sense and see a shimmering, suspended flame behind your dreaming eyes. As you focus on this flame, you ask Brighid to guide you in knowing what will best assist you right now in shedding this old skin and emerging in the one most fitting for you at this time. She responds by showing you a symbol in the dancing fire. When you see it, you ask Brighid to tell or show you how to use this symbol. You commune with her until you have received her guidance. Once you have, return to your body in your space with a deep, cleansing breath, open your eyes, and end your meditation with gratitude: *Many thanks to you, Brighid*.

Journal everything you have received, set your offering outdoors, and either put out your candle or let it burn out, whichever works best for you. During the day, contemplate how your received symbol and guidance relate with how you answered the meditation's opening questions, then practice putting your guidance to use. Feel yourself beginning to move toward the growing light that will be Spring's awakening.

Second Sunday – Brighid the Smith

Last Sunday, you rested in the dark earth with the serpent in the knoll, hibernating in the cold while dreaming of summer. To prepare for spring's emergence, you, like the serpent, shed that which was no longer needed, which had grown too tight and outworn, no longer fitting properly or feeling right. Now that the old skin has been shed, the serpent is freed and ready to rise.

Over this and the following two Sundays, the sleeping serpent of wisdom will slowly rise from its knoll within you, up through your inner cauldrons, just as the sun slowly rises over the faery hill, climbing a path of growing illumination leading to the triumph of emergence.

This Sunday, the serpent awakens and uncoils, and begins its upward ascent through your inner energy centers. As it begins

109

to rise, you will encounter Brighid the Smith and her Forge.

Before you begin, ensure you are prepared with an offering for Brighid, five fresh candles in your Advent candle holders, matches or lighter, and your journal and pen. If your candle holders are arranged with four on a perimeter and one in the center, save your central candle for Imbolc morn.

Welcome Brighid by leaving an offering on her shrine and lighting two of your five advent candles with the Flame-kindling Prayer:

Brighid,
Excellent, Exalted One,
Bright, golden, quickening flame –
Shine your blessings on us from the Otherworld –
You,
Radiant fire of the Sun.

Take three deep, slow breaths to center and ground yourself, then perform the Mantle of Brighid exercise to fully open yourself to her energies

Advent Work: The Forge

The way forward is both a calling and a making. Brighid calls our spirits to act in the world the way the sun bids our bodies to rise and walk out into the day. And after that, we must make each step ourselves along the sunbeam dancing on the ground before us. We must continue lifting our feet, putting one foot in front of the other, while trusting that we are still following the path, even when clouds obscure our way.

What inner resources will you call on to forge your path forward each day? What kind of life would you like to forge for yourself? What must you forge anew to best help you along?

Open your journal, ponder these questions, and note your responses. Then close your eyes, clear your mind with three slow, deep breaths, and open your inner sight to the following vision.

See yourself standing before Brighid's forge. See the bright fire, the shining anvil, the tub of water nearby, and her tools and implements ranged all around. As you breathe in, you smell the smoke, then take a step closer to the fire and gaze into its white-hot coals and ask Brighid to show you an image of a tool that can help you in your forging work. You breathe deeply and gaze into the coals until an image takes shape and you see the tool you need. Then look around and use the implements and supplies there to forge this tool in the forge's fire before you. Brighid guides both your mind and hands, and you find that you know exactly what to use and what to do. As you work at the forge, your tool takes form. Soon your tool is complete, and you stand back and admire your work. Taking a breath, you pick it up and hold it once again, then ask Brighid to show you how to use it. You listen quietly for her guidance and hear her voice speak within you.

When you have received what you need, take a deep, cleansing breath to return to your body and your space, open your eyes, and end your work with gratitude: *Many thanks to you, Brighid.*

Journal everything you have received, set your offering outdoors, and either put out your candles or let them burn down, whichever works best for you. Spend the day practicing using your tool as you have been guided. Feel how the light is beginning to grow both outside and within you.

Third Sunday – Brighid the Healer

Last Sunday, you visited Brighid's forge and engaged in co-creation with Brighid the Smith, creating, with her guidance, the tool she showed you that would best help you forge yourself and your life as you rise into the waxing year.

This Sunday, the awakened inner serpent is further uncoiling and ascending within you. Your focus this week will be within your second inner cauldron, the Cauldron of Motion. Here you will encounter Brighid the Healer directly at her healing well.

Before you begin, ensure you are prepared with an offering for Brighid and five candles in your Advent candle holders, matches or lighter, and your journal and pen.

Welcome Brighid by leaving an offering on her shrine and lighting three of your five advent candles with the Flame-kindling Prayer:

Brighid,
Excellent, Exalted One,
Bright, golden, quickening flame –
Shine your blessings on us from the Otherworld –
You,
Radiant fire of the Sun.

Take three deep, slow breaths to center and ground yourself, then perform the Mantle of Brighid exercise to fully open yourself to her energies.

Advent Work: The Well

The shedding work released you to move freely into the dawning year, and the tool you received and made at the forge allowed you to make our way forward. Now you must ensure that your path isn't impeded by shadow forms hungry for your energy, which will deplete you and your faculties for clarity, discernment, and deep understanding. As ever, the light thrown from Brighid's torch illuminates both that which had remained hidden and your way forward, which often lies within.

What fears most arrest your inner development at this time? Where do you feel this fear residing within you? What does it feel like? How does it manifest in your body? Is it connected to any health concerns you presently have? What might your life look like if you were released from these fears, were you able to repossess your energy locked up in them?

Open your journal, ponder these questions, and note your responses. Then close your eyes, clear your mind with three slow, deep breaths, and open your inner sight to the following vision.

See yourself standing before Brighid's Well. You see a clootie tree standing nearby, covered in colorful strips of cloth, and the many votive offerings left there for Brighid. You notice the damp smell of the earth and feel the chill of the wintry air. A cold breeze sweeps across your face and you hear it rattle the bare branches around you as it sends gray clouds drifting across the white sky. No one else stands at the well to overhear you, so you speak freely to Brighid. You tell her about the fears you carry and ask for her healing. You feel her compassion and love enfolding you as you speak, and you breathe it into your heart. When you have spoken all your words to her, you step forward and peer into the deep waters of the well. In response to your request for healing, Brighid shows you a symbol to use for your healing work.

Once you have received the symbol, you pick up a nearby cup beside the well and dip it into the water to fill it, then ask Brighid to tell or show you how to use this symbol to best heal your fears and return their trapped and renewed energies to you. You take three sips of the water and receive her guidance. When she has imparted her wisdom to you, take a deep, cleansing breath, return to your body and space, open your eyes, and end your work with gratitude: *Many thanks to you, Brighid.*

Journal everything you have received. Set your offering

outdoors and either put out your candles or let them burn down, whichever works best for you. Spend the day practicing using your symbol as you have been guided. Feel the power of the light waxing in strength as Spring draws closer.

Fourth Sunday – Brighid the Poet

Last Sunday, you visited Brighid's Well and communed with Brighid the Healer to assist you in facing the dark barriers of inner wounds that would impede your clear way upward out of the mound and forward through the year. The symbol you were shown and directions you were given for its use provided a medicine and a balm for your pain which you can carry with you and use should any new wounds arise.

This Sunday, at the precipice of the opening of the mound, the cresting of the light, the dawning of the fully waxing year, you will stand before Brighid's Flame of Inspiration as you engage with Brighid the Poet, who will show you how to bring together your work from the previous weeks and weave them into an act of power to accompany you on your journey forward into the year. Before you begin, ensure you are prepared with an offering for Brighid, five candles in your Advent candle holders, matches or lighter, and your journal and pen.

Welcome Brighid by leaving an offering on her shrine and lighting four of your five advent candles with the Flame-kindling Prayer:

Brighid,
Excellent, Exalted One,
Bright, golden, quickening flame –
Shine your blessings on us from the Otherworld –
You,
Radiant fire of the Sun.

Take three deep, slow breaths to center and ground yourself, then perform the Mantle of Brighid exercise to fully open yourself to her energies.

Advent Work: The Flame of Brighid

You have come so far: you have named your restrictions and shed them, created a tool to forge your way into the coming year, and divined a symbol to heal the inner wounds that would have sapped your vital energy. Now, on this final Sunday of Imbolc Advent, Brighid's Flame of Inspiration will shine its light on the new life waiting for you so you may glimpse your possibilities and the delights they promise.

Consider the shed skin of what you left behind on the First Sunday and what you are now released from to move toward. Consider the tool you forged and how it will help you make your way through your new life. Then consider the healing symbol you were shown and how, through its use, your wounded energies are now freed to fully empower your journey and keep your energy flowing should it again become bound up in dis-ease.

Now consider: *What might your life look like moving forward from this work of preparation? What will you do now that your restrictions are released, how will you do so with your new tool, and how will it feel with your healed and recovered energies? What shape does this new life take? And how does it feel?*

Record your responses in your journal, then seat yourself comfortably, close your eyes, and center yourself with three deep breaths. Now open your inner sight to the following vision.

See yourself standing on the hazel tree-lined banks of the Well of Wisdom, the otherworldly pool where the mythic Salmon of Wisdom lives. In the falling gloaming as the sun sets, you look down and see a light glowing from beneath the water. As you watch, it gradually approaches from the depths until a peak of flame slowly breaches the surface of the water and rises into a full blaze until it rests, silently floating above its reflection in the pool beneath it. You are standing before Brighid's Flame of Inspiration.

As you gaze upon Brighid's Flame, you call up the feeling inside you that you felt as you contemplated the new life waiting for you. As you do, a single word arises from the flame that perfectly encapsulates the energy of this feeling. It comes quickly and with little thought, as inspiration does. You say it aloud three times so its vibration will fully ring through all your layers of body, mind, and spirit. You know that this is your Word of Power for your coming year and new life, vibrating with the energy that you will be walking into as Brighid returns to and walks the land at Imbolc.

Looking down, you notice a hazelnut fall from one of the nearby trees, and watch as the pool's water fizzles and turns a reddish-purple hue. You reach down and scoop the floating nut from the surface of the water, crack it open, then place the shelled nut in your mouth. As you slowly chew it, you ask Brighid to tell or show you what kind of container you can best create to embody and express your Word of Power, whether a poem, song, musical composition, drawing, painting, or other creation that both represents your Word of Power and conveys its feeling from your vision.

When you have received her guidance, take a deep, cleansing breath to return to your body, open your eyes, and end your work with gratitude: *Many thanks to you, Brighid.*

Journal everything you have received, set your offering outdoors, and either put out your candles or let them burn down, whichever works best for you. Spend the day creating your container for your Word of Power so Brighid may bless it when she returns on Imbolc. The advent of waiting and preparation will soon be over and it will be time to celebrate Brighid's return. Feel how her light and power are ready to burst forth!

Imbolc ~ Brighid's Day
Brighid's Return

Your time of preparation was spent in seeking guidance in the dark of the earth, and then at Brighid's transforming forge, healing well, and flame of wisdom. Through these encounters, you have discovered tools to help you move forward and the knowledge of how to use them, then created an object to contain all this collected wisdom to become a touchstone for you as you move into and through the awakening year. Finally, after communing with Brighid for weeks in in the otherworld, she is coming to you as she returns to land and hearth to bless you and your home for the coming year!

In the Irish tradition, people sometimes leave a ribbon or a piece of cloth outside for St. Brigit to bless, called Brighid's Ribbon or Cloak, that they then use throughout the year for healing when someone in the home is unwell. For your flametending practice, you can set out a ribbon, scarf, or shawl for Brighid to bless so you can then wear it while keeping your flametending vigils and Brighidine seasonal celebrations, to help you further open to and connect with her energies. An object regularly used in this way will also collect and build power, which will further enhance your communion with Brighid. Consider the colors and patterns of the ribbon or fabric and how they speak to meaningful associations with Brighid, and/or symbols she has revealed to you in your communion with her during your vigils and fire festival meditations.

As the Scottish tradition includes tidying hearth and home in preparation for Brighid's return, take some time before Imbolc to dust and tidy your shrine and image or icon of Brighid to clean away the old year's energy and refresh it for the incoming energies of this new cycle of growth.

Imbolc Eve

On the night before Brighid's Day, bring your Word of Power

creation to your Advent shrine and don your Ribbon or Cloak of Brighid. Make a grain offering like bread or beer to Brighid to thank her for the sustenance of the last harvest that saw you though the winter. Then light your central advent candle, or whichever candle you have designated for Imbolc, while recite the Flame-kindling prayer:

Brighid,
Excellent, Exalted One,
Bright, golden, quickening flame –
Shine your blessings on us from the Otherworld –
You,
Radiant fire of the Sun.

Sit before your shrine, wearing your Ribbon or Cloak of Brighid, and holding your Word of Power creation, then settle yourself with three deep breaths and perform the Mantle of Brighid exercise. When you have completed it, simply rest in and absorb the energies of Brighid. As you do, speak freely with her to tell her about your Word of Power creation and what it means to you. Her energies filling and surrounding you will bless and empower your creation. Then sit quietly to make room for her to respond with whatever special guidance or wisdom she has for you, however she may do so. After a time, when you have received her response, bring yourself back to your body with three deep breaths, then slowly open your eyes. Finish your work with thanks: *All praises to Brighid.*

Journal Brighid's response to you and everything that you recall from your communion with her. Then extinguish the candle or let it burn down, whichever works best for you and set your offering outdoors. When you take it outside, find a place on a tree or shrub near your door on which to place your Ribbon or Cloak of Brighid, to be blessed by her Imbolc morning light. If you have no such ideal place, you can leave it on or near your

Advent shrine instead.

Imbolc Morn

When you wake the next morning, smile and rejoice, for Brighid and the season of spring have returned! Dress and prepare yourself, and ensure you have five advent candles ready in their candle holders and matches or lighter to light them. Step outside to retrieve your Ribbon or Cloak of Brighid and to recite this traditional Scottish Sun Prayer to welcome Brighid back to the land and sun as the energy of renewal and growth:

> Hail to you, O Sun of the Seasons,
> As you traverse the lofty skies!
> Your way is strong on the wing of the heavens,
> You are the glowing Mother of the Stars!
> You have your lying down in the destroying ocean,
> Without harming, without fear.
> You rise on the serene hillcrest,
> Like a Queenly Woman in bloom! *

When you come inside, light all five of your Imbolc Advent candles with the Flame-kindling prayer:

> Brighid,
> Excellent, Exalted One,
> Bright, golden, quickening flame —
> Shine your blessings on us from the Otherworld —
> You,
> Radiant fire of the Sun. *

Place a dairy offering to her beside her image to welcome the incoming bounty of the year. While the candles are lit, settle yourself and perform the Imbolc Meditation from the previous chapter, wearing your Brighid's Ribbon or Cloak as you do.

When you are finished, allow all the candles to burn down if you can, then set your offerings outdoors. Your soul is ready to embark on a new annual spiritual journey. *All praises to Brighid!*

*N.B. Items marked with an * are found in and/or inspired by traditional Gaelic lore and prayers found in* The Carmina Gadelica *by Alexander Carmichael.*

Epilogue

Transformation is Perennial

The universe constantly renews itself through cycles in which it makes, unmakes, then remakes its energy into a variety of forms. We see this in the turning of the seasons, the phases of the moon, the regeneration of plant life, and the life cycles of stars and galaxies. The process is never-ending because it is the way energy moves. Our souls are made of this energy, and so they too constantly ride the waves of this cycle. If you hold to reincarnation, then the cycle works through our lifetimes, but even without that and within this single lifetime, we learn and grow and change through experience. When experience is entered into consciously and deliberately, we can affect our own transformation and guide its trajectory.

Fire inherently transforms when it changes something through burning it, and like the phoenix, our eternal souls can repeatedly rise from the ashes of our illusions and obstructions that we choose to burn down in order to remove them from our path. In this way, we confidently forge our way forward and shape ourselves and lives with decisive action, then fortify ourselves so we are strong containers for receiving wisdom. Every change we choose strengthens our souls and our inner sanctuaries of spirit so that we are tempered to withstand greater challenges and grow to greater inner power.

Brighid is an apt guide for such a journey, and if looked to, her torch will guide, inspire and fortify you along your way by showing you how to embody her power to steer your ongoing transformative process. Flametending can be engaged with as a spiritual path and daily practice of transformative growth and enlightenment. I hope these pages have inspired you to step into this practice to see how you can, with Brighid's guidance, be an agent of your own spiritual development. May her strength, healing, wisdom, and vision be with you.

Please feel free to follow me on Facebook and chat with me about these journeys with Brighid at https://www.facebook.com/authorerinaurelia.

Forge
by Erin Aurelia

Hammer and tongs in hand,
   I settle myself at the forge

the fire is built, the bellows have
   blown, and the ore stands ready,
      poured into forms resembling

joy and fear
   security and confidence
      comfort and chaos

the power of the hammer
   must now shape them
      like bones
      like limbs
   and I feel each blow on
      my skin
   as I fashion the form I wish
      to take, and shape the life
         I wish to live

molten gold becomes my
   marrow as I glow from
      within from a secret flame

and I speak with a tongue of fire as
   poetry flows from my head like a
      river of lava, creating the land
         where I will live

and all those who also burn with
   love and truth and mirth and grief
      may join me here—

on this island of coals

floating

on a cosmic sea

Appendix

Flametending Orders

These orders are open to those seeking to practice flametending with a dispersed community. Some accept women only; some are co-ed or gender nonspecific. Some are geared toward pagans and polytheists and some are nondenominational, open to Christians and pagans alike. Solas Bhríde is the physical home of St. Brigit's Flame where candles lit from its wick can be ordered so you may tend Brighid's Perpetual Fire in your own space.

Clann Bhríde
https://clannbhride.org/fellowship/clann-bhride-cill/

Daughters of the Flame
https://www.obsidianmagazine.com/DaughtersoftheFlame/

Nigheanan Brìghde
https://www.facebook.com/groups/nigheananbrighde

Ord Brighideach
https://www.ordbrighideach.org/

Solas Bhríde
https://solasbhride.ie/meeting-rooms/

References

Carmichael, Alexander. *Carmina Gadelica.* Lindisfarne Press. 1992.

Laurie, Erynn Rowan. *Ogam: Weaving Word Wisdom.* Megalithica Books. 2007.

MacKillop, James. *Dictionary Of Celtic Mythology.* Oxford University Press. 1998.

MacLeod, Fiona. *The Winged Destiny: Studies in the Spiritual History of the Gael.* Duffield & Co. 1911.

MacLeod, Sharon Paice. *Celtic Myth and Religion: A Study of Traditional Belief, with Newly Translated Prayers, Poems and Songs.* McFarland & Company. 2011.

Meyers, Kuno, translator. *Miscellanea Hibernica.* University of Illinois. 1917.

Monaghan, Patricia, editor. *Brigit: Sun of Womanhood.* Goddess Ink. 2013.

O Duinn, Seán. *Rites of Brigid: Goddess and Saint.* Columba Press. 2005.

O hOgain, Daithi. *Myth, Legend, and Romance: An Encyclopedia of the Irish Folk Tradition.* Prentice Hall General. 1991.

MOON
BOOKS

PAGANISM & SHAMANISM

What is Paganism? A religion, a spirituality, an alternative belief system, nature worship? You can find support for all these definitions (and many more) in dictionaries, encyclopaedias, and text books of religion, but subscribe to any one and the truth will evade you. Above all Paganism is a creative pursuit, an encounter with reality, an exploration of meaning and an expression of the soul. Druids, Heathens, Wiccans and others, all contribute their insights and literary riches to the Pagan tradition. Moon Books invites you to begin or to deepen your own encounter, right here, right now.

If you have enjoyed this book, why not tell other readers by posting a review on your preferred book site.

Find more titles and sign up to our readers' newsletter at
http://www.johnhuntpublishing.com/paganism
Follow us on Facebook at https://www.facebook.com/MoonBooks
and Twitter at https://twitter.com/MoonBooksJHP